"Thank God for Alan Noble—for his voice and witness! Like all of Alan's books, *To Live Well* is a balm for the hurting, written with honesty, wisdom, and so much love. How can we piece together all the fragments of advice in our oversaturated world? *To Live Well* puts the puzzle together for us, cementing the broken bits of colored glass into a cathedral window through which we experience God's light."

Jessica Hooten Wilson, Fletcher Jones Chair of Great Books at Pepperdine University and author of *The Scandal of Holiness*

"We live in a culture marked by restlessness and chaos, in great need of clarifying voices. Alan Noble is one of those voices. *To Live Well* offers us the gifts of astute cultural insight, pastoral steadiness, and practical help, reminding us that human flourishing isn't a reality we construct but is found in returning, again and again, to the One who offers us life and life to the full."

Jay Y. Kim, pastor and author of *Analog Christian*

"There are certain writers who seem to come at their topics from different directions than I do yet reach the same conclusions. Alan Noble is one of these writers, which is exactly why I find such pleasure in reading what he writes. In this book, he writes as someone who has studied his subject deeply and loved his readers well. It is philosophical yet practical, profound yet understandable, and always deeply biblical. I think it's just what many young Christians need to grow their obedience to God and spur their love for others."

Tim Challies, author of *Seasons of Sorrow*

"What a book! Each chapter brims with wisdom—drawn from Scripture, steeped in deep reading, and refined through life experience. I found myself not only nourished personally but also earmarking pages to send to family and friends wrestling with major decisions or simply trying to make faithful daily choices. Truly one of the year's best."

Trevin Wax, vice president for resources and marketing at the North American Mission Board and author of *The Thrill of Orthodoxy*

Foreword by Justin Whitmel Earley

An imprint of InterVarsity Press
Downers Grove, Illinois

InterVarsity Press
P.O. Box 1400 | Downers Grove, IL 60515-1426
ivpress.com | email@ivpress.com

InterVarsity Press® is the publishing division of InterVarsity Christian Fellowship/USA®. For more information, visit intervarsity.org.

Published in association with the literary agent Don Gates of The Gates Group, www.the-gates-group.com.

Cover design: Faceout Studio
Interior design: Daniel van Loon
Cover images: © Valeriya Simantovskaya via Stocksy

ISBN 978-1-5140-0224-7 (print) | ISBN 978-1-5140-0225-4 (digital)

Printed in the United States of America ♾

Library of Congress Cataloging-in-Publication Data
A catalog record for this book is available from the Library of Congress.

33 32 31 30 29 28 27 26 | 13 12 11 10 9 8 7 6 5 4 3 2 1

Dedicated to my students who have taught me

the meaning of virtues every day.

CONTENTS

FOREWORD

Justin Whitmel Earley

IN *THE ABOLITION OF MAN*, C. S. Lewis wrote that the task of an educator is not to cut down jungles but to irrigate deserts. That is exactly what Alan Noble accomplishes in this book.

Most people I speak with today are not lacking in ideas. We are quick—perhaps too quick—to adopt ideologies. But when it comes to actually living, we are lost. We stride through life like confused farmers, brimming with theories even while staring at barren fields, puzzled that our clever ideas yield no fruit. By re-introducing us to the traditional virtues, Noble begins to lay the much-needed pipes of irrigation.

Like you, I want to live well. I want to make good decisions and do the right thing, even when it's hard. But how to choose wisely (prudence), how to act justly (justice), and how to persist courageously despite adversity (fortitude) are questions that elude us, even though history has already answered them quite well. Our modern world has simply forgotten—or ignored—them.

That is what makes this book such a gift. Recalling writers such as Aristotle, Jacques Ellul, Josef Pieper, and T. S. Eliot, Noble brings us back to the virtues with fresh insight, reminding us of what we already knew but had left behind. I found myself rethinking how I make decisions, and why I so often lack confidence in them. I thought about why justice and politics have gotten so confused, and what the ancients would have thought about how I think about my neighbor. I was reminded why love must animate all of them, lest they be worthless.

And yet—and this is important—I thought about none of this with guilt! Because the book you are about to read points over and over to the grace that secures our salvation while also showing how that same grace is the basis for living well.

I suggest you read with a pen; I took a lot of notes. Better still, read ready to practice.

INTRODUCTION

FOR MOST OF US, somewhere along the path to adulthood comes the unsettling realization that most people are winging it. They don't know what they are doing. They don't know where they are going. And they aren't sure what the point is. To some extent this is just the challenge of growing up and figuring out life, but there is something special about the modern world which has disoriented us and our moral imaginations. We lack guiding principles and authority figures to orient us toward the Good Life. Near the beginning of T. S. Eliot's *The Waste Land*, he diagnoses the problem, telling the reader, "You know only / A heap of broken images."[1] Which is kind of insulting but true, if you think about it for five seconds. Although Eliot didn't have TV or social media in mind, our lives are made up of broken images—billions of broken images that don't fit together into a coherent whole, except maybe one loud message that says: "You Aren't Good Enough. Buy Stuff and Work Harder."

Eliot didn't just have images in mind, however. He was also thinking about ideas. And our ideas are broken too. The messages we receive about how to live, what to live for, what my identity is, how to love, who to love, what it means to be a good person, what careers to pursue, what justice is, what my obligation to my neighbor is, who my neighbor is, what my ethical responsibility is to someone I can't even visualize who lives across the globe and who mines the rare earth metals for my smartphone—all these messages conflict. They don't make sense. If we were to try to live out the life that our teachers, the state, the experts, our doctors, the scientists, our therapists, our life coaches, YouTube gurus, and our friends told us, we would drop dead from exhaustion.

All we have known is a heap of broken images. So naturally most of us are winging it.

When this hits you—and if it hasn't hit you, it will—you'll probably start looking around for some wise older person for help. And I wish I could tell you that you'll find that person and receive the mentorship you need to navigate this ridiculous world. But from personal experience, those people are hard to find. They exist. I know they do, but there are not a lot of them. Because we live such fractured and alienated lives, it is difficult to have deep, meaningful, long-term relationships with people—the kind of relationships that are necessary for good mentorship. And the reality is, this isn't the first generation to live with a heap of broken images. Keep in mind, Eliot published that line in 1922. Your parents' generation and grandparents' generation and great-grandparents' generation all lived with a heap of broken images; we just have the (significant) added burden of technology, which fractures our lives even further.

Of course, you can find plenty of people who will give you recommendations for optimizing your life. There's a lot of money in self-help. But it's just more broken images. One guru tells you to exercise more. Another tells you to hustle harder. Another tells you to meditate. Another tells you to find a meaningful job. Another tells you to find yourself. Another tells you to get some new form of therapy. And once you finish listening to all these coaches, you end up feeling more drained and inadequate than when you started. Oh, it may work for a while, but the crash comes, eventually.

And that's the thing. For some people it feels like the broken images *are* enough. You can piece together a life of significance and meaning by selecting the fragments that suit you personally. You take a little consumerism, add a dash of Christianity, a pinch of romanticism, and a smidge of healthy living, and if you don't stop moving, you can stay afloat and feel largely fulfilled and content. But eventually life catches up. Life gets difficult. Addiction overwhelms you. Tragedy strikes. Suffering comes, as it does to all of us. And the patchwork quilt of a life you've pieced together no longer seems that secure anymore. You need something more solid, more substantial, more coherent. You need something sufficient to the task. We all do.

This would all be easier to deal with if you could just stop caring so much, if you weren't passionate about living a life of meaning, but you *do* care. You've been told to care. And while you may doubt a lot of the broken messages tossed at you by contradictory sources your whole life, the one thing that has always made sense is that your life *ought* to matter. Life is too hard, too painful, too wonderful and crazy and beautiful and intense. There's too much potential and grandeur for it to not mean anything—for your life not to count.

For those of us who are Christian, the meaning is provided in our faith already. And that helps a lot. Our lives matter because Jesus died for us, and the meaning and purpose of our lives is to serve, enjoy, and honor him. That sounds wonderful in the abstract, but when you only know a heap of broken images, when you only know a thousand different career options and a million different ways of ministering, when you are even unsure who you *are*, it can be hard to see how that faith *practically provides guidance for your life*. You won't admit to having this insecurity in Sunday school, but you think about it while driving home.

Life feels like a mess, a heap of broken images that don't cohere, don't make sense, and you care too much to give up. And unless you are one of the few blessed with a wise mentor (not all mentors are wise, I'm sorry to say), you probably feel alone in this. The question is, How can you survive? How can you get through? How can you live rightly in this chaotic world? The challenge is to live well. To pull together the pieces that *do* fit together, the images that belong, the ideas that are true and good and beautiful, so that you can rightly see the image of God.

I don't know this for certain, but I think Eliot's heap of broken images is a shattered stained-glass window that would have depicted a scene from the Bible, maybe the crucifixion, maybe the resurrection, maybe the ascension. Maybe all of them. Such a scene reminds us of God and his character, and therefore our relation to him and how we were created to live for him. At the time he wrote *The Waste Land*, Eliot was not a Christian, but he understood that the loss of Christianity in the West was the loss of coherence. And I think we're still feeling the effects of that loss a hundred years later. I think you are still feeling the effects of it, even if you were raised in the church.

One of the most significant aspects of this "loss of coherence" has been the denial of human *telos*, the creational design to our lives that gives us direction and purpose. Instead of believing that we all share a purpose in glorifying God and enjoying him forever,[2] modern people are left to discover their own purpose, to define their own nature. This leads to fractured and contradictory messages about what the "Good Life" is and how to reach it. That's one reason we feel so confused and conflicted in the contemporary age. What we will discover in the coming chapters is that when we accept we were designed to live for God's glory, *how* to live begins to make sense.

So, what I want to suggest is a way to gather up the pieces that make up the Way. The purpose of this book is not to go over the basics of the Christian faith, or to explore the gospel in detail, both of which are beautiful and essential tasks, they just aren't my task here. Instead, I want us to look at the traditional virtues, the ways of walking that are the natural and proper outcome of the Christian faith: prudence, justice, fortitude, temperance, faith, hope, and love. My fear is that modern society has conditioned us to be full of "morality"—albeit a shifting and ambiguous morality—but lacking in any virtues because it denies that we have a *telos*. As a result, we are anxiously striving to do the right thing but never sure what the right thing is.

Virtues are cultivated habits that align us with who God created us to be. God made us to love, so when we cultivate the virtue of love, we become more fully who God made us. We pursue these habits, not to become righteous before God, but because we have Christ's imputed righteousness and are adopted children of God. The Holy Spirit enables us to practice these virtues so that we might bring glory to God as we were created to do.

Historically, church fathers and theologians have appealed to the virtues as important to the Christian life, from Saint Augustine and Thomas Aquinas to Reformers like John Calvin and Niels Hemmingsen. Although there has not always been agreement about what makes up the list of virtues, one of the strongest traditions comes from Aristotle through Thomas Aquinas, listing the four cardinal virtues (prudence, justice, fortitude, and temperance), to which Christian thinkers, like Aquinas, added the three theological virtues (faith, hope, and love). It is possible to talk about other virtues (for example, humility), but I believe these seven are the essential ones and that most other virtues fall under one of these. As we shall discover, the beauty of the virtues is that they offer a biblically and historically grounded way of living in a chaotic modern world.

But this isn't a book of easy answers ("The Bible says: Don't have sex outside of marriage," which is true, by the way), but practices and postures of living that allow us to make sense of the world, to cut through the confusion of messages and pressures so that we know how to live, so that we don't have to feel so stuck all the time.

These practices are going to be hard; I should warn you about that. In fact, our primary scholarly guide to the virtues, Josef Pieper, himself failed to live up to the highest standards of justice and fortitude when the Nazis came to power in his home country of Germany. His opposition to the National Socialists was not as clear, pronounced, and forceful as it could have been.[3] Pieper acknowledged his inability to live up to the high standards of virtue in the preface to one of his books, writing that he was "utterly unable to meet" them.[4] For all of us, the pursuit of virtues is hard work. And as we will discuss in the conclusion, all of us will fail in this life to some extent or another. But through the work of the Holy Spirit and the grace of Jesus, the God who began a good work in us will bring it to completion (Philippians 1:6). Our ultimate sanctification, including in the virtues, will be brought about by Christ, but our duty today is to be faithful to heed the call to practice wisdom, even when it's hard.

Contemporary life is already hard and overwhelming. Meanwhile, Christ's yoke is light. It is still a yoke, but it is light because we have the help of the Holy Spirit. You're going have to die to yourself, but dying to yourself is a whole lot better than being suffocated by restlessness and confusion. Because under Christ's yoke there is grace.

My goal is to walk through the essentials of life.

We will consider: How do you choose what to do with your life when surrounded by endless options and pressured with the obligation to Change the World? As we'll see, the answer is not to find the One True Career or to wait patiently for God to give you some special revelation, but to choose *something*, something honoring to God and for the common good of your community, and then do it. Maybe it only works for a time and you end up doing something else next year (or even next month), but when you are faithful to do something good rather than anxiously trying to do the One Right Thing, you will find peace. And more importantly, you'll honor God.

Next, we will look at the controversial and timely issue of justice. There may be no other topic of our time with more broken, contrary images than the topic of justice. Everyone has an opinion on what matters most and what you must care about. In some spaces, you can get shamed for not immediately announcing your disgust with some current event. In other spaces, you can get shamed for not signaling your allyship or support for someone's chosen identity. The question of what is ethical, what is just, and what is loving easily gets lost in the noise and fervor of the moment. But that is no excuse to ignore justice.

Christ has called us to do justice wherever we are, to whatever extent we are capable. Whenever it is in our power to do good, we are required to do so. That's an astonishing and startling commandment. And yet, there it is (I told you I was going to ask you to do hard things). We will look beneath the usual culture war hot topics, look beneath the appearances of justice to see what Christ is calling us to, what our right obligations are, and how we can practice those in a world that demands everything of us all the time.

Few people will tell you this, but life involves a lot of suffering and therefore requires a great deal of courage or fortitude. It involves way more suffering than we expect—unless we've already experienced it. And even then, there's probably more on the way. This is a hard saying, but it's true. History, literature, religion, philosophy, and the humanities have all taught this truth as essential for right living. Life is not exclusively suffering, but you'll experience a great deal of suffering in this life.

We will explore the reality that you are going to suffer greatly in this life, and you need a plan to deal with that suffering through courage. Through the scriptural understanding of suffering as producing endurance and through comprehending how to deal with suffering, we will discover a better path than the contrary and incoherent messages of this world.

We will explore the problem of excess. From our earliest moments, we are trained to desire anything and everything. Our entire economy is based on a system of consumption. Even if you think of yourself as self-controlled in your spending, you have been exposed to the idea that your desires are good and you should say Yes! to them your whole life. (And not just by advertisements.)

Every product in the grocery store calls out to you. All digital devices call out for your attention. Authority figures will encourage you to affirm your assumption that *everything* in our world seems to be about you and for you, and it all seems to say the same thing: Your desires are good, and you should say Yes! to them. With such constant and consistent programming, it is almost certainly the case that it is harder for us to say No! to our disordered desires than many people in the past. We learn the practice of temperance, of choosing not to do all that we can do for the good of our neighbor and the glory of God. And it's going to be a lot harder than you think.

When Christians think about challenges to their faith, they tend to think about philosophical or apologetic challenges. What do we do about the creation story? How do we make sense of apparent contradictions in the Bible? How can free will and God's sovereignty coexist? How is hell just? And so on. These are good questions deserving of good answers—and I will provide none of them. Other people have answered them. In fact, the church has addressed these questions for thousands of years. Instead we will consider deconstruction and the doubts that plague every believer throughout history. Is it possible to "deconstruct" your faith and remain Christian? How do you live with doubts about your faith? What happens when you grow bitter toward God over suffering? Does that mean you lack faith?

We will wrestle with the question of hope in a divided, chaotic, violent, and frankly quite depressing world. While there are certainly pockets of progress, there are also mass shootings, increasing suicides, polarization, creeping authoritarianism, addiction to pornography and digital devices, escapism, boredom, endless wars, endless culture wars, church abuse scandals, and worse. As with personal suffering, we have to know how to deal with the horrors of the world. How do we not lose hope when everything seems utterly out of our control? I have seen people fall into despair over climate change. And I understand. It *is* distressing to watch our environment change in ways that harm people and nature. As with all of these topics, we receive contrary and overwhelming messages from different forces in society, all demanding our passion, attention, devotion, and money. And we can't solve these problems by ourselves. In some cases, I don't even know how we can solve them collectively without God's intervention. But here's the thing, we serve a God who does intervene, who has intervened, and who calls us and even commands us to hope all things. Isn't that remarkable?

Finally, we will consider the greatest difficulty we face in life: how to love rightly. We intuitively know that love is at the center of life's purpose, but what is it? How do we love? It's not always clear. As with each of these topics, we have inherited from culture a heap of broken images of love—love as lust, love as individual fulfillment, love as unconditional acceptance, love as emotion, love as intuition, love as sacrifice, love as romance, love as 1 Corinthians 13, and so on. As we will discover, love is simpler, more complex, more demanding, and more glorious than we can imagine. Love is the proclamation, "It is *good* that you exist; how wonderful that you are!"[5] Love is the practice of desiring the good of other people, which begins with knowing what the good is, and the good is a Person.

As we move through each virtue, our model will be Christ. And our guide for this journey will be the renowned Thomas Aquinas scholar Josef Pieper, who has explored the seven virtues in two books, *The Cardinal Virtues* and *Faith, Hope, Love,* and is considered to be "one of the great Catholic philosophers of the last century."[6] At times I shall have occasion to diverge sharply from Pieper's Catholic theological conclusions, but Pieper has much wisdom to share with Protestants. Pulling from his profound knowledge of Aquinas, Pieper explicates each of the virtues with theological and philosophical rigor. Our task will be to make Pieper's insights a relevant light to the contemporary world. Writing from the 1930s through the 1970s, Pieper's essays on the virtues have been widely praised. Pieper not only explains Aquinas's position, but elaborates on it with his own views as a Catholic philosopher. Other great theologians and philosophers will join our journey, including figures like Aristotle, Augustine, and John Calvin, who wrote in his *Institutes of Christian Religion* that he did not intend to write on each of the virtues, but that readers should look instead to other writers and to the homilies of the early church fathers.[7] It is my hope that in some small way this book might be numbered among those other writings on the virtues Calvin recommended.

Piecing together the broken stained-glass window is difficult but not impossible. Once we are done, we will still be surrounded with broken images that call out to us, demanding our attention, pressuring us, condemning and accusing us. But as we are grounded in the image of God and reminded of how that image guides us in this world, we don't have to be restless and confused. Fixing our gaze on God and using the cardinal and theological virtues, we can put together a coherent image of how to move through life in the modern world, one that responds to difficulties like shifting notions of justice, wisdom, morality, and love. In practicing these virtues through the work of the Holy Spirit, we gain freedom from sin and from the power of a chaotic world.

1

CHOOSING DECISIVELY

One of the most difficult aspects of life is making choices, and the modern world has given us endless choices. It seems like the first fourth of our life—roughly until the age of twenty-two—most life choices are made for us. We live on autopilot. Most of us, at least. We are forced to go to elementary, middle, and high school. We are compelled or guilted to go to college or trade schools. Then during those early twenties, most of us are presented with two massive, future-defining choices: What kind of career will we have and who, if anyone, will we live with?

The answers to these questions will determine the success, shape, and nature of the rest of our lives. And we are reminded of the weight of these choices, *repeatedly*. Yet neither choice is a simple matter of personal preferences. Both our career and the marriage and friend pools are fiercely competitive. Everyone is fighting for a limited number of jobs in rapidly changing fields, thanks in part to AI. Everyone is fighting over a limited number of available, eligible, and desirable spouses and friends. And time seems to be running out. The older you get, the less options you have available and the more pressure you feel from your family and friends to "get on" with life, which puts you into an impossible position. On the one hand *everything* apparently rides on you making the one right choice in trade or major or career or spouse or friend. On the other hand, there are so many possibilities and so many variables to consider that you are frozen, unable to choose anything at all.

Perhaps you fear missing out on something or someone. You like the idea of going into nursing, but you also enjoy psychology. You are in love with someone, but you are also interested and attracted to someone else. If you marry someone tall, you'll never have the pleasure of being with someone short. If you marry someone, will their career goals conflict with yours? Is it worth giving up your career goals to be with them?

But there's another, more insidious pressure that people feel over making the Right Life Choice. These choices don't just shape our lives, they can come to *define our existence.* And this is where things get really intense. If finding the right career determines my career satisfaction, that's one thing. But if it determines whether my life has meaning? That's something else entirely. Now every major life decision is an existential decision. In a culture where meaning, value, and purpose are defined by the individual, each person is burdened with creating and sustaining an interesting, exciting, and enviable life. The burden of your existence has been placed on your shoulders by society. So you aren't just looking for the right spouse. You're looking for one who can save your life, who can redeem you. You aren't just looking for a job, you're looking for a calling that can justify your place in the world—a vocation that provides you purpose and significance. The goal of life is to become the Best Version of Yourself, and you do this by making the choices the Best Version of Yourself would make. You have to make the *optimal* choices, because you only get one shot at this!

And then choice paralysis sets in. The more choices we have and the higher the stakes of those choices, the harder it is for us to make any choice at all and the less satisfied we are when we do make a decision. When there are only a few options available to us, our choices come easier. When those choices don't matter very much, we find it easier to choose. But when everything hinges on these choices among millions of options, well, don't mess up! As a result, we freeze, unable to make any decisions, big or small. The world is too overwhelming and the stakes are too high. This is what I mean when I reference T. S. Eliot's lines that we know only "A heap of broken images."[1]

To navigate such a world, we need to cultivate the virtue of prudence.

PRUDENCE DEFINED

When Jesus turns water into wine in John 2:1-11, we can see him modeling prudence. The story begins with Jesus and his disciples attending a wedding feast and his mother coming up to him with a loaded comment: "They have no wine." Jesus recognizes the implicit request in this statement, but he responds with an objection: "Woman, what does this have to do with me? My hour has not yet come." Mary does not directly respond to him, and instead tells the servants to "do whatever he tells you." At this moment, Jesus has to use prudence to make a decision. As he has already stated, his "hour has not yet come." It's not time for him to start doing miracles in public. And yet that fact conflicts with the fifth commandment: Honor your father and your mother.

To navigate this moment, Jesus must assess the reality of the situation accurately, deliberate for an appropriate amount of time, make a decision, and act decisively. While we don't get to see Christ's internal process of deliberation and decision-making, we know that he was conflicted between his ministry schedule and his obligation to his mother, and he ultimately made a decision. His decision is that he is obligated to obey his mother, and so he orders the servants to fill jars with water which he then turns into wine. Notice that once Jesus makes up his mind, he acts with singleness of purpose and without any comments about how he "really shouldn't be doing this right now, since my hour has not yet come." He makes a decision and he acts decisively. That's prudence.

There are different ways of understanding the virtue of prudence, but at its essence prudence can be defined as making the right decision at the right time. Wheaton College philosophy professor W. Jay Wood defines *prudence* as "the act of thinking truthfully about the best means to appropriate ends."[2] Notice the three qualifications in this definition: thinking *truthfully* about the *best* means to *appropriate* ends. To make prudent (and therefore virtuous) decisions in life, you must accurately assess situations, make a choice based on what is the good, and choose means to achieve that good end, which are themselves good.

Saint Augustine famously defined prudence as "love distinguishing with sagacity between what hinders it and what helps it."[3] For Augustine, prudence is a matter of recognizing and choosing those things that lead to a more righteous life. And Josef Pieper, drawing from Aquinas, argues that prudence is the mother of all moral virtue, the foundation for justice, fortitude, and temperance.[4] Prudence should not be conflated with *wisdom*, which is a broader and richer concept in Scripture. Wisdom gives you understanding of Scripture and God (Proverbs 2:1-5), whereas prudence teaches us how to make day-to-day decisions.

For our purposes, I want you to think of prudence like this: Prudence involves (1) seeing the reality of a situation, (2) recognizing and desiring what is good, (3) deliberating, (4) making a judgment, and (5) resolutely acting on that judgment.

REALITY

The first step in making a prudent decision in life is making an honest, objective assessment of the situation, whether that be choosing a major in college, selecting a roommate, or deciding whether to spend time scrolling on your phone (also a matter of *temperance*, which we will discuss in chapter four!). This process of seeing the reality of a situation includes practical things like researching, finding facts, seeking information, asking for clarification, and recalling accurately. If you cannot see a situation accurately, you cannot act. So we must see rightly before we can decide rightly before we can act rightly. But seeing rightly isn't as easy as it might seem.

For one thing, our pride and biases often hinder us from seeing reality as it is. We might imagine we are being objective when really we're allowing our preconceived notions to color our vision. No one can be perfectly objective, but we can cultivate attitudes and postures toward the world which bring us closer to reality. For example, Pieper warns, "A closed mind and know-it-allness are fundamentally forms of resistance to the truth of real things."[5] If you come to a decision with a closed mind, you will not see "the truth of real things" and therefore you will not make a prudent decision.

The Christian philosopher Esther Lightcap Meek describes this posture in terms of respect: "Knowing never stops requiring our submission to and respect for the real."[6] Practically this means that in the process of making a prudent decision, we should pray and ask God for clarity, for help to see the nuances of the issue with open eyes, for the humility to submit to reality whatever it may be. To choose prudently requires that we remember situations honestly, we consider the situation with an open mind, and when something unexpected happens, we don't jump to conclusions. It means setting aside our biases to see a situation for what it *is*, not what we anticipate or hope or expect. As with all aspects of virtues, this takes practice: the continual effort of choosing to set aside your ego and presumptions and fears to survey reality for what it truly is.

In her book *A Little Manual for Knowing*, Meek argues that we love to know. Loving someone or something is the way we know rightly, because in the process of knowing we pledge ourselves to the task of knowing and we trust ourselves to the process. Knowing, in Meek's account, is more than just the collection of data, although it includes information. Knowing is relational and intentional. It involves a particular posture of the whole person. It requires humility and openness before the object of knowledge. It requires the suspension of assumptions, which so easily limit our perception of the object.

In day-to-day life, an openness to the otherness of an object of knowledge involves humility. When you struggle to *know* where you ought to live, you stay open to the possibility that God will lead you to live in a strange place, a place well beyond what you have imagined as suitable for you. In our rush to know for sure, we close off possibilities, which prevents us from seeing reality as it is. Meek agrees with Pieper and Aquinas that prudence (in her language, knowledge), involves rightly seeing reality.[7]

While there is value in exercises like making a pro and con chart when making a difficult life decision, Meek's description of knowledge suggests that true knowledge is deeper and more intimate than a list of facts. It begins with a posture of our hearts.

Once we have determined what the reality of a situation truly is, by loving to know, then we can pursue the good. But what is "the good"?

DESIRING THE GOOD

Built into Pieper's conception of the virtue of prudence is that it is always oriented toward the good. Notice how similar this is to Solomon's words: "The fear of the LORD is the beginning of knowledge" (Proverbs 1:7). Unless we recognize God's sovereignty, we cannot begin to make prudent decisions. This is how biblical wisdom (a knowledge and fear of God) is an essential prerequisite for true prudence.[8]

The assumption here is that there *is* a good, an external, authoritative standard by which we can evaluate our actions. This is a controversial claim for the contemporary world where it is assumed that individuals have their own, private, self-defined good. Christians identify this good in the great commandment: loving God and loving our neighbor (Matthew 22:36-40). Or put differently, as the Westminster Shorter Catechism does, the "chief end of man" is to "glorify God, and to enjoy him for ever."[9] The first thing to notice here is that this understanding of the good is expansive. There are an almost infinite number of ways to glorify God in our lives. There are an almost infinite number of ways we can love God and love our neighbor as ourselves. How does desiring the good bring us closer to making a decision about who to marry or what career to pursue?

The flaw in this line of reasoning is the idea that the good always refers to the One Right Choice, when in fact, once we understand the good as glorifying God and enjoying him, it turns out there are lots of *good* choices we can make in life. What's key for prudential thinking is that we take the good into account—that we intentionally look for what will glorify God in our choices. Often that will leave us with *several* options, and there we have the freedom to select among those options.

But this only pushes the problem back one step further: If the good is loving God and neighbor or glorifying God and enjoying him forever, what does it mean to do those things? How do I know what is loving to God and my neighbor? How do I know what glorifies him? This is where the daily practice of dwelling in the Word is so important. It is in the work of the Holy Spirit ministering to us, especially through the reading and interpreting of the Word of God, that we come to understand what it means to love him. Through the practice of reading and meditating on Scripture, particularly in a local community of saints, we come to know how to love God and our neighbor. We learn more about his character and how to glorify that character. The prudent person has immersed themselves in the Word and in a local church community, which helps them interpret that Word in order to know the good in any particular situation.

It is not enough to merely consider the good; we must desire it. According to Pieper, "Only one who previously and simultaneously *loves* and *wants* the good can be prudent."[10] Just as we must pray for humility and clarity of sight to see reality rightly, we must also pray for a heart that desires what is good. And because God is a loving Father who cares for his children, he will grant that request, giving us, over time, a love for what is good through the process of sanctification.

Pieper goes on to note that the more we practice prudence, the more our love for the good will grow, which in turn better enables us to be prudent. Love of the good is positively reinforced by prudence.[11] In this life we are going to get habituated to something. Society calls us to be habituated to our passions, to what our flesh defines as "good": lust, distracting entertainment, excessive material possessions, political animus. The reality is that whatever habits we cultivate become easier, more desirable, and more important in our lives. They shape our identity. The only question is whether you will cultivate habits of imprudence and ignore reality and the good, or prudence and come to accept reality and love the good.

DELIBERATION

Once you have assessed the reality of a situation and cultivated a desire for the good, the next step is to deliberate carefully on what end you ought to work toward and what means you ought to use to reach that end. According to Aristotle, deliberation must focus on what we can actually *do*.[12] So in situations where there is no action for us to take, where there is no decision for us to make, we must learn to trust God and his providence.

Deliberation is where many of us get stuck. We spin our wheels deliberating and never come to a final judgment on a matter. In a hectic and frantic world, we are often urged to make rapid decisions without contemplating reality or the good. And sometimes we must make rapid decisions, but too often in our society we make hasty decisions because of sales pressure or peer pressure or impulsivity. The basis of deliberation is careful contemplation of the reality of a situation and the goods involved. Paul talks about this in Romans when he calls us to discernment: "Do not be conformed to this world, but be transformed by the renewal of your mind, that by testing you may discern what is the will of God, what is good and acceptable and perfect" (Romans 12:2). Although Paul doesn't use the word "prudence," he is describing it. The problem is, who can know the will of God? How can we deliberate properly? Part of the answer is that we don't do it alone.

According to W. Jay Wood, "The first 'phase' of prudential reasoning requires that we seek the wise counsel of others."[13] This of course is a biblical concept: "Where there is no guidance, a people falls, but in an abundance of counselors there is safety" (Proverbs 11:14). This is especially important, as Aquinas points out, because life is so complex; there are so many different situations each of us will face that having a variety of prudent elders to counsel you can be invaluable.[14] But Pieper makes the point that the ultimate decision is always up to the individual. There is no way you can deputize someone to make a choice for your career or marriage or any life decision for you. In the final analysis, you are the one responsible. And the reason for that, argues Pieper, is that no one else can see the reality of your situation exactly like you can.

Pieper does have an exception to this rule, however. He argues that when you have a prudent friend who loves you, they can help shape your decision from inside your ethical dilemma by imagining themselves in that situation.[15] This is one of the most comforting passages in all of Pieper's writings to me. It's true that no one can step into my shoes, but a true prudent friend who knows me deeply can help shape my decision by putting themselves in my situation. This speaks to the need we have to make deep, lasting, meaningful friendships with virtuous people. There have been many times in my life when my own mind has led me astray and I have had to rely on the prudence of a friend to shape my thinking. Such are moments of God's grace to me, and I don't take those relationships for granted.

But this kind of relationship requires a certain posture of the heart, a humility and even a submission to someone wiser than yourself. In her *Little Book of Knowing*, Meek describes the relationship this way:

> A guide is only as effective as our decision to trust and to submit to that guide. We make a responsible choice to trust what they say even when we do not understand or agree. We cannot be suspicious or noncommittal about this. We have to be willing wholeheartedly to try out what they recommend. Apart from this that guide cannot help, and our investment does not pay off. Submission and trust are not the same as mindless compliance. They don't actually even require agreement. They involve another critically important, sophisticatedly human, covenantal "let there be." They involve free personal consent. Submission and trust aren't always comfortable. But they are necessary to knowing.[16]

In addition to receiving the prudent guidance of a trusted friend, we must have our own humility to accept their wisdom. And as Meek points out, this isn't always comfortable, but it is good.

Wise guidance can be explicit or it can be imitative: "Prudence on our part sometimes shows itself in having the good judgment to identify and imitate the morally wise among us."[17] Either way, the prudent person should cultivate a group of friends and wise elders who they trust to give counsel and act as models of prudence. This entails knowing people for an extended period of time, watching them navigate life with wisdom and prudence, making godly choices in a variety of difficult situations so that you have reason to trust their counsel. Of course, even wise counselors can give bad advice, so it is sometimes prudent to seek a few different voices. In our American society, we tend to rely exclusively on our own intuition and opinions, but prudence calls us to trust in the wisdom of others as we deliberate a serious decision.

Whether we rely on wise guidance from others or not, we need to spend time deliberating ourselves. This means a quiet time of contemplation and reflection, thinking through the reality of the situation and what the good is. The ultimate guide for our deliberations is the Holy Spirit, and so in any situation we should pray to God for wisdom, for the clarity of mind to think through the issue at hand in a way that glorifies him.

JUDGMENT

At the end of the day, whatever ethical decision we face, we have an obligation to come to a judgment about what the prudent course of action is. Life is infinitely complex, and while some people would like you to believe that there are nice, tidy answers to all of life's problems, that is not reality. The decisions we have to make are nuanced and specific, which is one reason why cultivating the virtue of prudence is so important. If the Bible were simply a clear guidebook on how to respond in every situation, then we could just turn to the right chapter and verse, get our answer, and move on. Instead, the Bible mostly gives us the foundational principles that we must apply with the aid of the Holy Spirit. And that is the practice of prudence.

The more we practice prudence, the more we discover that it requires flexibility. This is rooted in the fact that prudence, at its core, is about seeing the world as it really is. And the world "as it really is" is a mess—a profoundly complex living system that defies our ability to create simple legalistic boundaries. We have to be agile and nuanced in our thinking to make prudent decisions, recognizing the complexity of the world. In the case of a career, it would be nice if I would just tell you the five steps to discovering and achieving your goals. But there are no nice simple steps. There is only a mess of individual experiences, talents, skills, constraints, economies, technologies, and so on. We wrestle with reality, keeping the good in mind, and trust in God's providence.

We also need to accept that God has grace for our mistakes, because we are going to make wrong choices in life, and some of those mistakes will cost us and others greatly. This is an unavoidable part of living in a fallen world. We make judgments about how to act and people suffer as a consequence. And while we should do what is reasonable to right the mistakes we have made, ultimately we cannot fix all the mistakes we make in this life. At some point we have to accept God's mercy and grace. We have to accept that he is sovereign and caring for everyone involved in our decisions. Our duty is to practice prudence as best we can with the aid of the Holy Spirit and rest in God's providence. But the key is that we must come to a decision. We cannot allow timidity to keep us stuck. We must leave the stage of deliberation and decide what to do.

RESOLUTE ACTION

Aside from getting stuck in deliberation, many of us get stuck in following through with our decisions. We decide to move to a new state, and then never follow through with the plans. We decide to exercise, but never go to the gym. We decide to make new friends, but never make human contact with anyone. Prudence is not a virtue if it is not executed with resolute commitment. Recall the model of Jesus when Mary asked for his help at the wedding feast. He acted resolutely.

As Wood states, "To know what to do, and to fail to act, whether due to fear, weakness of will, or some other cause, is to fail in in [sic] the most important part of prudence."[18] Notice how similar this is to the warning in James 4:17: "Whoever knows the right thing to do and fails to do it, for him it is sin." When we come to a prudent decision, we have a moral obligation to follow through with unwavering action. And according to Pieper, the decision to act comes *before* we have "absolute certainty."[19] In our risk-adverse society, making mistakes is viewed as a mark against our personhood rather than a normal part of living. We want that absolute certainty that we are marrying the right person or choosing the right career. But that kind of certainty doesn't exist. We each make the best judgments we can, and then we act with resoluteness, committing to our decision with our whole hearts and accepting the consequences of our actions, whatever they may be.

The prudent person is known not only for their wisdom, but for their *actions*. Prudence is something you *do*. You make an unwavering commitment to follow through with your judgment, trusting in God's sovereignty and the Holy Spirit–guided deliberation you made. This requires another virtue, fortitude, or courage, to act with confidence in your decision. Not haughtily or pridefully, but with full knowledge that you carefully considered the reality of the situation, desired the good, deliberated with wise counselors, came to a judgment, and now are acting resolutely. This is what it means to be a prudent person: "The virtuous agent must act in full knowledge of the end being sought, must choose to act for the sake of the end and not from impulse, and do so from a firm and unchanging character."[20]

PRUDENCE APPLIED

Careers. When we begin to consider what career to have, we typically weigh three questions: Am I good at it? Can I support myself? Do I enjoy the work? These are all appropriate questions that help us get to what the "good" is. It is good to find a career you are skilled at, that can pay you enough to live on, and that you take some joy in.

God has created each of us with skills, talents, and aptitudes and given us opportunities to develop them so that we can flourish as we work, whatever that work may be. As we practice *seeing reality for what it is*, it's important that we take honest account of our skills. Some people flatter themselves and imagine they have skills they do not really possess. Others hide behind false humility or low self-esteem so that they don't recognize their skills. Here we should rely on the insight from trusted counselors about what our abilities are, and if we discover that we don't have marketable abilities, we must do the practical work to cultivate them. Just because you can't easily identify a marketable skill does not mean that you are hopeless. It just means you need to devote more time to evaluating yourself, choosing a skill, and developing it.

One critical mistake people make is in adopting the standards of the world in regard to what is a respectable career. As a result, we can come to look down on some skills, talents, and aptitudes as less significant and others as overly significant. For example, it's not uncommon for young Christians to see ministry or missions as the *ideal* vocations. As if a formal career in ministry would sanctify your life in ways that "secular" vocations could not. We forget that God is the one who sanctifies us, not our career choices. Seeing *reality* for what it is means seeing *beyond* society's expectations.

Another aspect of seeing reality is taking into account the potential to pay your bills and give generously to others. While the love of money is the root of all kinds of evils (1 Timothy 6:10), it's also true that money can be used to bless others. So it's not even inherently selfish to desire a well-paying career. At the very least, you ought to take an honest look at the economy and evaluate which careers will pay enough for you to provide for yourself and others.

Finally, it's good to find work that brings you pleasure. All work is laborious by definition, but not all work is *drudgery*. A good job will fill you with a sense of the purposefulness of your labor and satisfaction at a job well done. Those feelings can carry you through the times of drudgery. The key is that your labor must have some definite, meaningful end. Jobs which require you to work without a clear, obtainable goal that helps someone in some way tend to drain us. We can work them for a time, but only a time. This standard means that you can do what is referred to as "menial" labor and find great fulfillment or do highly technical labor and feel empty. What matters is the purposefulness of the work. That's what will give you long-term satisfaction.

For example, knowing that your work in a grocery store is helping to feed families with healthy foods while treating them with respect and dignity as full human beings can be deeply satisfying work. Your labor *does* something meaningful. Whereas realistically, some occupations just ask us to produce meaningless objects that don't serve the good of our neighbors and end up in a landfill somewhere. I can think of many mobile phone games, for example, that are incredibly mindless, addictive distractions designed to get people to spend money they don't have. There is nothing redemptive or loving about such careers, there is no deeper purpose, and therefore nothing deeply satisfying about working these jobs.

As important as these three questions are, we need to add a fourth: Is this work *good* for my neighbor and honoring to God? The theologian Richard Baxter made this point when he declared: "The *publick welfare*, or the good of many, is to be valued above our own. Every man therefore is bound to do all the good he can to others, especially for the Church and Commonwealth: And this is not done by *Idleness*, but by *Labour*!"[21] You may be particularly skilled at the designing of video gambling machines—a career that I'm sure pays well and which brings you deep satisfaction as you invent, design, and build new machines—but since your work will only be a drain on the lives of others, this is not a worthy pursuit. It's neither honoring to God nor is it edifying to your fellow image bearers. On the contrary, it preys on their addictions and ruins lives.

The rest of the world is going to fervently insist that the main goal of a career is to bring personal pleasure. Sometimes this pleasure takes the form of the satisfaction that your labor will "change the world." But too often "changing the world" is just a corporate slogan to justify greed. After all, social media "changed the world" and that came with profound global mental health consequences. Personal pleasure can't be the ultimate good for Christians who are pursuing work. We are called to love our neighbor with our labor, and anything less than that standard is unacceptable. This goes beyond a "do no harm" ethic, where we choose a career that suits us and then ask if it harms our neighbor in some measurable way. Instead, the effect of a career on our neighbors should be the *first* question we ask as we survey reality. And doing so will mean that we have to reject jobs and careers that otherwise we might embrace.

These four questions make up the good of work, but not all of these questions have equal importance. There may be times in your life where you need to work a job that brings you no immediate joy but which pays your bills, blesses your neighbor, and is one at which you have some skill. Understanding these priorities is the definition of prudence. Or you might work a job that barely pays your bills but gives you great personal satisfaction and is a significant benefit to your community. When considering a job, ask the questions in this order:

1. Is this good for my neighbor and honoring to God?
2. Can I support myself on this salary?
3. Am I gifted in the skills necessary for this job?
4. Will this job bring me deep, meaningful satisfaction?[22]

Once you answer these questions, you can successfully weed out many potential careers, and the problem of choice paralysis is reduced somewhat. But realistically, in the West, most of us are still going to have many career options available. You have surveyed the reality of your career options, you have identified the good of work, and now this is where the real work of choosing shows up.

You must learn to accept that you have many good options, and you can't choose them all. There might be three great careers open to you, or within one career you might get five great job offers. More likely, you'll receive two job offers that involve considerable tradeoffs and one graduate school acceptance letter. Both jobs meet all four criteria, but they require you to move away from friends and family, or to take a pay cut, or accept new, daunting responsibilities. It's not uncommon to experience having many potentially good options for life choices and yet none of them are without significant tradeoffs. Remember that Jesus had to use prudence to decide between the good of his ministry schedule and the good of honoring his mother. He made a judgment and acted resolutely.

Weigh the tradeoffs, count the costs, deliberate with wise counsel, but *make a judgment and rest in it.* Don't worry about missing out on other opportunities or closing doors by opening a door. If you are not your own but belong to God—and you do—then your life is not validated and vindicated by making the Right Life Choices. You aren't looking for the One Right Career to justify you. So you have the freedom to make a choice, follow through with it, and see where it leads. Be resolute. Choose something that honors God, blesses your neighbor, pays your bills, involves your skills, and brings you satisfaction, if you can, and go with it. Realistically, you won't know whether it will bring you real satisfaction until you've worked a job for a few years. You won't even know how skilled you are at it until you have time to develop those skills. In other words, you can't be certain. You can never be certain, but you don't have to be. Remember what Pieper said, you must act *before* you have "absolute certainty."[23] You just need to look at the real-world information (as opposed to what we imagine) and make a resolute decision.

Maybe you'll get it wrong. That's okay too. This needs to be stressed. It's okay to choose the wrong job or to get stuck in the wrong career path for a while. You'll survive it. Many people try a career for a while and shift into a new field when it doesn't work out for them. In fact, you're not going to be good at your career when you first start out. That's normal. Keep at it. But if it doesn't work for you after a reasonable amount of time, it's okay to move on.

This kind of flexibility is especially important in a fast-changing economy. If you can start a career and stay in it for forty years, that's wonderful, but most of us will have to change careers at some point. Accepting that makes it easier for us to choose a career in the first place. Yes, you will never get the time back if you start a career in marketing and have to restart for a career in medical billing, but you are never starting from square one. The experiences you had in your first career will be valuable for your growth as a person and specifically as an employee even if the new career field is radically different.

Hold your career loosely. Devote yourself to your work. Work heartily unto the Lord, but accept that a career is not a covenant. We'll consider when it's prudent to move on from a commitment at the end of this chapter.

One of the most meaningful and fulfilling career choices you can make is to not pursue a traditional career at all, but to be a stay-at-home parent. Or maybe you stay at home to care for your aging parents or grandparents or an ill relative. If the world's career standards are correct, then sacrificing your prime working years to care for another human being is a massive waste of potential, and what we really should do is devote ourselves even more intensely to our careers and pay someone else to care for our children, parents, or our sick family members. But the world's standards aren't oriented toward the good, so they are not prudent. Instead of caring for someone else being a waste of opportunity, it is the fulfillment of some of our most human drives and capabilities. We have the ability to sacrifice our desires and preferences for the good of others. We can do that in a career or by opting out of a traditional career altogether.

I don't bring this up to guilt anyone who chooses to use childcare or assisted living for the elderly. Instead, I want to open up the possibility of not using those services. In most cases this practically means living on a single income, lowering your standard of living, and devoting most of your time to caring for humans. I think that our culture has swung so far in the direction of independence and self-achievement that for many people the idea of staying home with children, the elderly, or the sick is unimaginable. Collectively, we need to make these basic human practices imaginable again. And that starts with normalizing these choices and honoring those who make them. There are many subtle ways in which we tend to minimize or denigrate those who choose, or are required, to stay at home. We expect a certain standard of living for everyone and are surprised when those living on a single income fail to meet that standard. We subtly shame those who can't participate in the solidly middle-class lifestyle.

In the evangelical church it's fairly common to praise stay-at-home mothers as the model of motherhood while also treating stay-at-home mothers as socially boring. This is, after all, the impression society gives us—what is interesting is the workplace. What is interesting is making money. How much money you make tends to define how prestigious your job is, which tends to define how interesting you are. This is deeply ingrained in our culture. But this ought not be so.

Particularly within the church, the choice to forgo a career and financial gain in order to care for another human being ought to not just be praised as virtuous in the abstract, but as *interesting*. People who make this choice should be perceived as compelling, fascinating, vibrant contributors to a community, because they are. But that is often not the case. I want to do something difficult here. I want to advocate on the one hand for being a full-time caregiver and admonish all of us to elevate our estimation of caregivers, while on the other hand I want to acknowledge that those who choose this path will almost certainly be treated unfairly. Your work will be minimized. Your perspectives will be trivialized. You will be perceived as boring and unimportant by a significant part of our community. On top of all this, you will suffer a loss of income. I'm sorry. This will be the burden some of you must bear for a time. But know that your work is important, that you are interesting and worthwhile. And do the good work before you anyway, in devotion to God. Do it resolutely. And do what you can to surround yourself with people who see your value and the value of your labor. Support and encourage each other in your works.

A similar thing could be said for many careers. There are many careers in the modern world that are valuable, meaningful, and important but are denigrated or dismissed as trivial. Choosing to work as an elementary school teacher in a public school does not come with much prestige, but the work you are doing is so important. The same can be said for electricians and plumbers, mail carriers and lawn care professionals. There is great dignity in your labor if you labor unto the Lord and to the edification of your neighbor. If we practice our faith rightly, churches should be alternative spaces where occupations are not honored based on the cultural prestige or income they generate, but on how they honor God and love our neighbors. If the prudent career for you is one the world denigrates, do not take that into account. Make the prudent decision and you will be rewarded.

Marriage. Choosing a spouse is not like choosing a career. Marriage is a covenant for life, whereas careers can change multiple times. But some of the same pitfalls face us in choosing a marriage partner. We experience the same pressure to find The Right One and the same idea that through it we can find existential justification. Some of this we will deal with in the seventh chapter, which focuses on love as a virtue. There we will consider the nature of love and how to love well. But here I want to focus on the *prudent choice* to love someone specific for life.

Since there is so much confusion about what marriage *is*, I think it's helpful to begin by establishing what we are talking about before we begin seeing the reality of a romantic situation. Instead of first asking what the reality of any specific relationship is, we can ask, What is the *good* of marriage? What was it created for? Part of the answer is that it is "not good that the man should be alone" (Genesis 2:18). We were created for community, and while some people will choose to fulfill that need for community through friendship and singleness (which is a God-honoring choice!), the primary means God created to meet this need is through marriage between a man and a woman. God also says that Eve was created to "help" Adam. So part of the purpose of marriage is mutual aid through this difficult life. Everything from practical help managing a household to emotional support and spiritual encouragement—we all need these things from someone, whether it is a close friend or a spouse.

In marriage we enact a living metaphor for the relationship between Christ and his church, this is another part of its *good*. Through marriage we learn in an embodied way about Christ's love for his church. We learn what it means to sacrifice for one another, to care for the spiritual life of another. Of course it is not necessary to be married in order to understand this metaphor, but I do think that there is a level of embodied understanding that comes through marriage, just as farmers better understand farming parables in the Bible.

In marriage God has provided for the continuation of his creation through procreation. Children should be seen as one of the main purposes of marriage. This is part of the *good* of marriage. Not an incidental personal preference that you use to decorate your life or marriage, but at the core of married life. This doesn't mean that all married couples will have children. For medical reasons and other extenuating circumstances there are situations when it is not wise or possible. But it does mean that those in the church should view parenting as a central purpose of marriage. It is one of the ways we are "not our own" in this life. We belong to our children and our spouse. As with getting married, there is no "right time" to begin having children. You'll never be "ready" for the reasonability, the burden, and the joy. It is a miracle which you accept as a gift from God, and you shepherd that gift with prudence.

Marriage between a man and a woman is also the one place where sex finds a proper expression. Here both spouses care for each other and are drawn into a closer one-flesh union with each other.

Now that we see what the good of marriage is, we are ready to look at the reality of a romantic situation. Our goal here is to look for a fitness for marriage. When I say "fitness for marriage," I don't mean that you must be *certain* that you are "ready" for marriage. Most of the best things in life you have to jump into without being fully ready. You can't be truly ready until you jump. This is true for having children, for example. Instead, I mean that you have sought wise counsel from elders and friends who have encouraged you that you have the character to be in a lifelong, committed relationship right now.

Remember, the key to prudence is seeing reality as it is and making a committed decision based on that. There are several aspects of a potential marriage that you should examine before you make a commitment. It may be that there are major areas of maturity you need to work on. Take an honest assessment of your spiritual maturity, your responsibility, your ability to deal with conflict, your readiness to apologize and admit mistakes—these are elements of personal maturity that you should survey in yourself with the help of close friends and loved ones. After you have checked the reality of your own fitness, you ought to consider your potential spouse. What are their weaknesses? How do they respond to criticism? Are they willing to apologize and admit their mistakes? Are they committed to the Lord? How do they handle adversity? These are important questions to ask. Your goal is not to find *perfection*, but to see reality as it is. Recognize their faults and flaws and sins, not out of spite or condescension, but out of prudence. You are not marrying to save someone, but to form a union.

Once you have assessed the fitness of you and your potential spouse, you need to consider the reality of living together. Can you afford it? Where will you live? If you can afford to pay your bills and find housing, then money should not hold you back. Often people allow a middle-class standard of living to define what is acceptable, which prevents them from getting married or having children for fear of "missing out." As a result, they miss out on marriage or having children. Be prudent, but don't be held back by demanding middle-class standards of living. School should also not prevent you from getting married in most situations. Getting married while in college is quite doable. It may be hard, but it's doable. Waiting for the "optimal" time to get married (or have children) may mean you hesitate indefinitely.

Don't get married just because you want to have sex and you feel like you can't control yourself. Even within marriage you must learn to live chastely. You don't get to have sex whenever and however you want in marriage. And there will be stretches, maybe even long stretches, when you can't have sex within marriage, even healthy marriages. Due to stress, health, travel, housing, children, and life in general, you'll have to learn chastity within marriage (we'll talk more about this in chapter four). You'll have to learn to live with burning passion, which means that the habits and practices you develop *before* marriage will be important for a healthy, righteous sexual relationship within marriage. And while I believe there is a great beauty in marrying young, I don't think marrying for the sake of sex is wise or loving. I have known more than a few marriages that ended badly because they were begun badly.

In marriage, as with all prudent decisions, resoluteness is a key. The prudent person sees a situation clearly (or as clearly as it can be seen) and makes a resolute decision, which means that they are not tossed about by every doubt. They make a choice, and they walk that choice out, facing the consequences of their decision, both good and bad. Resoluteness does not exclude the possibility of divorce in some tragic situations, but neither does it needlessly seek it. In a society that constantly reminds us that we have outside options, resoluteness is a sign of deep maturity and commitment, and it requires a profound faith in God and his providential guidance. Not a faith that we will only make the right decisions, but that God works all things together for our good, because we love him. Our task is to be people of our word, faithful to the choices we've made. Not quick to doubt or slow to commit.

Once you have done all this, will you have found the One Right Person for you? No. At least, not necessarily. Lord willing, you will have discovered someone you can build a beautiful, godly marriage with, but in all statistical likelihood, a better match exists for you somewhere out there in the world. And that doesn't matter. If you continue looking for the ideal option, you will choose nothing and you will grow bitter at the opposite sex. And after you get married, you will have to accept that you will meet interesting, beautiful people who could be wonderful spouses and you'll have to deny the urge to pursue them and remain committed to your vows. There's beauty in obeying the vows you have sworn before God to be faithful to your spouse. And there's beauty in the imperfection of your spouse.

Yes, you can imagine a better spouse, and maybe you even know of someone who embodies those desirable qualities (although I suspect they aren't as ideal as you believe!), but the spouse before you is beautiful in their uniqueness. This is one of the lessons of contentedness—that the frailness of the person or thing or situation before us is an opportunity for us to delight in its uniqueness. This is especially true of people. So, no. At the end of this process of prudent discernment, you probably won't find your One True Love (who is Jesus anyway), but Lord willing you will find a beautiful, imperfect spouse to spend your life with.

THE SUNK COST FALLACY

While prudence calls us to be resolute with our judgments, we still must be wary of what's called the "sunk cost fallacy." Being resolute does not necessarily require you to stay committed to a bad decision. That is not prudence. That is folly. Let's say you make a decision based on your best understanding of a situation, and you act resolutely to follow that decision through, but over time you come to see reality more clearly. And what you thought you knew no longer holds true. Prudence demands that you act on that new information rather than stay committed to a misguided decision.

The sunk cost fallacy is the belief that since you have already invested in a choice, it's better to stay committed to that choice even if you have evidence that it's a bad investment. For example, you may begin a relationship with someone and over time it becomes clear that the other person is not mature enough for marriage or children or a serious relationship, but since you have been with this person for six months or a year, you feel compelled to stick it out. That's the sunk cost fallacy. Or perhaps you choose a major in college and take several classes in that major only to discover that you lack any talent in that field and find no joy in your studies. The sunk cost fallacy is the belief that you must stay with that major and invest *more* time and effort into something that you are not good at and brings you no joy. Prudence asks us to reevaluate our beliefs when significant new information becomes available. That doesn't mean that we are constantly reevaluating our choices. But when significant new information becomes available, we weigh it against our decision and in community.

For most of us, the temptation will not be to stay committed to bad decisions, but to constantly doubt all our decisions, because we live in a society that constantly pulls us toward inconsistency, dissatisfaction, and doubt. We live in a society in which alternatives are always prized over contentedness, in which contentedness is equated with laziness, apathy, and a failure to pursue your dreams. Such an environment invites us to second-guess ourselves, to always be expanding, adapting, evolving, maximizing, and optimizing. The same spirit that drives corporate expansion drives our wills, if we allow it.

Prudence, in such a world, means balancing several competing values. Once again, it first of all involves an accurate, honest view of a situation. Second, it requires us to make a decision and act on the basis of that accurate view. Third, we must be resolute in our decision, not constantly wavering or flagging, but confident and oath-keeping. Fourth, we must be willing to reevaluate a decision if we come to understand that our view of a situation was not actually accurate. And all of this must be done with a view toward the good.

As we have seen in the examples of careers and marriage, the habitual practice of prudence can help us make difficult and important life decisions in a way that glorifies God and brings us joy. It can also help us make day-to-day life decisions that we might have been deciding on instinct, passion, or habit. We don't need to be stuck in the trap of choice paralysis. We have the freedom to act resolutely with the aid of the Holy Spirit. We just need to devote the time and have the courage to deliberate, desire the good, make a judgment, and act resolutely.

2

ACTING JUSTLY

OF ALL THE PROBLEMS FACING the contemporary person in the West, one of the most perplexing is the question of justice. How do we live together justly? What duties do I have to my neighbor? Who *is* my neighbor? What responsibility do I have to correct the injustices committed by my forebears? What responsibility do I have to correct the injustices committed by dead people in my country when my direct ancestors took no part in the injustice? What responsibility do I have to correct the injustices committed by people who look like me, share my race or gender or ethnicity?

Or what about the climate? Many people today are experiencing "climate anxiety" over the injustices being done to our planet and their limited agency to prevent the coming catastrophe. How can we live "normal" lives knowing that our environment is collapsing? How can we bring children into such a world? In an article for the *Los Angeles Times* titled, "It's Almost Shameful to Want to Have Children," author Jade S. Sasser interviewed several millennials and members of Generation Z to get their views on having children in light of climate change. One young woman answered the question by saying, "I know that things aren't going to get better. So why would I want to put a child through that? Even when my sister gave birth to my nephew, I was like, Why? They're gonna go through so much."[1] Why, indeed.

We could go on covering all the various justice issues plaguing our nation and filling our headlines and social media and often tormenting our consciences, but I'm not going to give you a list of issues for you to address. Instead I want to help you think through what justice *means*, how it ought to operate in our minds and in our habits.

It is particularly important to understand what justice *is* because the concept is used so flippantly today, especially in online advocacy. Everyone acts as though they know what justice is intuitively, but their definition usually amounts to *whatever I think is just*. This kind of moral reasoning has been titled "emotivism" by philosopher Alasdair MacIntyre.[2] We determine morality based on what feels right or what our preferences are. This, in a culture that exists *After Virtue*, as his book is titled, is what we have left. The book you are reading is a call *back to virtue*, and therefore away from emotivism, away from purely internal and exclusively subjective means of making moral judgments. We need a firmer foundation to determine what is justice than whatever our intuition, preferences, and emotions tell us. Because we are not our own but belong to God, there are standards for justice and we are called to align our values with God's values, even when it costs us dearly.

Emotivism can lead to all kinds of conflicting, emotionally charged justice claims thrown around by passionate advocates of causes, especially on the internet. This is the "heap of broken images"[3] we receive about justice. I have little doubt that this has contributed to the rise in anxiety among young people. They desire to be just and morally upright, but the world feels impossible to navigate morally, particularly if you are not part of a marginalized group. Because in addition to emotivism, power dynamics define justice in the modern world. If you wield power, you have privilege and therefore you must be oppressing and dominating another group. It's a secular version of the doctrine of total depravity without the doctrine of grace to redeem us.

We should stop and recognize a kernel of truth to both emotivism and this Marxist idea of power. It's true, for example, that our intuitions and emotions can *help* us make moral judgments. My disgust over the horrors of genocide is not irrelevant to my discernment that it is unjust. My empathy with victims of abuse is not irrelevant to seeking justice for them. The question is, how should my emotions affect my judgment? Similarly, power dynamics do exist and people in power often abuse their power to oppress people. Marginalized groups exist. That is a reality of existence, not a Marxist theory. The only question is how to justly treat those marginalized groups and how to justly wield power. The contemporary theory of justice seems to hold that power is inherently corrupt, but we will discover that true justice calls for a rightly ordered power.

JUSTICE DEFINED

In Matthew 22, the Pharisees thought they had caught Jesus in a trap over what was due to Caesar: "Teacher, we know that you are true and teach the way of God truthfully, and you do not care about anyone's opinion, for you are not swayed by appearances. Tell us, then, what you think. Is it lawful to pay taxes to Caesar, or not?" (v. 16-17). The Pharisees were hoping to force Jesus into saying it was not lawful, since Caesar's taxes were so burdensome to the Jews and since they were from a pagan ruler. Then they could accuse him of being rebellious. But Jesus saw through their trap and focused on what true justice is:

> "Why put me to the test, you hypocrites? Show me the coin for the tax." And they brought him a denarius. And Jesus

> said to them, "Whose likeness and inscription is this?" They said, "Caesar's." Then he said to them, "Therefore render to Caesar the things that are Caesar's and to God the things that are God's." (Matthew 22:18-21)

Despite the oppressive taxation that the Jews were experiencing and the fact that those taxes went toward an empire that was pagan and wicked, Jesus offers no excuses for justice. What is Caesar's belongs to Caesar. What is God's (everything) belongs to God.

Pieper, drawing from Aquinas, who draws from Aristotle, says that justice "is the notion that each man is to be given what is his due."[4] Elsewhere he describes it as "the intentional habit that enables man to give to each one what is his."[5] We are obligated by justice to give anyone whatever we owe them, including taxes to pagan Caesar. Justice is a virtue when it is done *habitually* and *intentionally*. Defined this way, much of life is a matter of justice. It is an injustice not to tell the truth because you owe your neighbor the truth. It is an injustice to steal because your neighbor is owed their own property. It is an injustice to have a broken refugee system because you owe the refugee a fair system to flee violence and distress. We owe a lot of people a lot of things. The obvious question is: *How do we know what is due to someone*?

Fundamentally, our due is determined by our rights, and as Pieper notes, our rights are determined by the created order. We are owed basic dignity and freedom because God created us:

> Man has inalienable rights because he is created a person by the act of God, that is, an act beyond all human discussion. In the ultimate analysis, then, something is inalienably due to man because he is *creatura*. Moreover, as *creatura*, man has the absolute duty to give another his due.[6]

It is in our human nature that we find the basis for justice in the basis of rights. One way of understanding this is through the language of belonging to God. We have rights because we belong to God. That belonging-to comes with implications about how others are to treat us. Because we belong to God, others are obligated to respect us as God's creation. We have the right to be free from abuse, neglect, violence, lies, theft, and other injustices.

Justice, then, is giving someone what they are due according to the rights given to them by God in the created order and the Bible.

Another aspect of justice is that it is a fundamentally *external* virtue. In other words, what matters for an act to be just is what you actually do or fail to do, not how you feel inside or what you intend.[7] You could intend to help the poor by cutting off the social safety net and forcing them to get jobs, but if that leads to children starving, you have done an injustice. Your feelings and intentions are irrelevant to whether an act is just, which doesn't mean that your intent doesn't matter. You ought to desire justice. Justice in the full sense involves both an internal will and an external action.[8]

The flip side of this is that all of our actions have implications for justice: "*Every* external act is of social consequence. We do not speak without being heard; we do not make use of a thing without using our own or another's property. It is justice, however, that distinguishes what is one's own from that which belongs to another."[9] This has profound implications on how we think about justice, because we like to think in hyperindividualist terms: I commit an injustice when I explicitly harm someone else; otherwise, my actions are merely my personal choice. But this is not the case. We live in community and all of our actions have broader social implications on matters of justice.

This communal understanding of justice, rather than the hyperindividualistic model we are used to, fits better with reality. Consider the effects of illicit drug use in a small town. A hyperindividualist perspective would say that those individuals are ruining their own lives or (more optimistically) choosing to live how they want. But their choice to destroy themselves will inevitably lead to further crime and abuse and neglect and harm. Even if these individuals manage not to commit further crimes, the very fact that they are not contributing to the common good of the community is itself an injustice. And this is another aspect of justice: We have an obligation to seek the common good. We owe the community our talents, skills, contributions, gifts, labor, love, wisdom, and (most of all) our witness to the gospel. If you have bad habits or vices, they creep into the community and affect everyone, whether you want them to or not. Part of justice is giving what is due to the broader community, which is you living a righteous, virtuous life.

THREE BASIC FORMS OF JUSTICE

Justice can be broken down into three basic forms, which are helpful for us as we sort out what modern justice looks like: legal justice, distributive justice, and commutative justice. Legal justice involves our obligations to obey the government. We perform legal justice when we give the governing authorities what is their due. Distributive justice is the government's obligation to us. We perform distributive justice when we are in positions of authority and properly administer goods to those who are owed them. Commutative justice is the justice owed between civil parties, between you and your neighbor.

Legal justice is fairly straightforward. Romans 13 gives us the basic understanding of how to follow legal justice: We are to submit to our governing authorities. Jesus modeled this for us when he rendered unto Caesar the things that were Caesar's. Where things get challenging is when those governing authorities command us to disobey God's commands, in which case we must choose to follow God rather than human authorities. As our country becomes more secular, I suspect that there will be more and more situations where Christians will be forced to decide between honoring the state's mandates and God's commands. But for now, in the United States at least, this is rarely a conflict.

On the issue of distributive justice, where the government distributes goods and services to citizens, Pieper notes that although the primary obligation is from those who can administer goods to us, we recipients also have an obligation to gratefully accept what is given to us.[10] Which means that while we can argue and protest about the lack of medical services provided by the government, we should also accept what is given to us with a spirit of gratitude. It turns out that having a grateful heart can be a form of justice!

One of the more interesting implications of what Pieper calls "*iustitia distributiva*" is that the community takes on an obligation for the growth of the common good: "all the good things bestowed in creation (men's capacities and abilities) belong to the 'good of the community,' and that *iustitia distributiva* entails the obligation of granting such abilities the protection, support, and fostering they need."[11] This means two things. First, that good gifts come from God from heaven and are given to individuals for the good of communities. It's not that the gift of painting or accounting does not belong to the individual to whom it has been given, but they owe the benefits of that gift to those around them.

In other words, your giftings are not your own. They belong to others as well. If you have been gifted with an ability to teach, you *owe* it to your community to exercise that gift to help educate others. As John Calvin writes, "the endowments which God has bestowed on us are not our own, but his free gifts, and that those who plume themselves upon them betray their ingratitude."[12] We owe them to our neighbors, not to making ourselves look good. If you have been gifted with the ability to sing, you owe it to your community to sing.

Second, the community owes something to the gifted individual: "protection, support, and fostering." In other words, there is a relationship at play here. Just as you owe the benefits of your gift to your community, your community owes you the ability to exercise your gift, the space to practice it, the education to mature it, and the encouragement to continue it. And the more support the community provides, the more benefits the gifted individual has to offer to others.

This might rub against our American individualism, but it is a brute fact of communal life. If the community does not foster the growth of artists, they should not expect artists to arise among them. Or at least, not very good ones. If the community does not invest in education, they must not expect future educators to arise among them. Reciprocally, if artists and educators abandon their communities, they must not be surprised when those communities are ungrateful and unsupportive.

Practically, this means that we should have the good of our neighbor in mind. We ought to desire them to flourish. It is not enough to discover your abilities and devote yourself to mastering them for personal gain. You owe it to your neighbor to invest in your abilities and their abilities. Sometimes this looks like monetary investment. It may look like going to a local play or buying the work of a local artist. It may look like giving piano lessons to local children or volunteering to help fix the plumbing in your church. But it also looks like properly funding and supporting schools so that children are able to foster their abilities.

Just distribution is done with a vision for the good of the community in mind, not out of selfishness or any personal ambition. At the same time, administrators of justice must have individuals in mind as well, not just masses of people. We should seek to elect administrators who humanize the work of distributing justly, focusing on the common good of the society and the reality of the life of the individual. The goal of *iustitia distributiva* is to give each person their share of the common good according to their dignity, ability, and capability.

As you can imagine this cannot be calculated in absolute terms on some actuarial table, which is why administrators must use prudence to make wise decisions. Part of our duty is to treat government administrators and bureaucrats as *real human beings* rather than as cogs in a machine. Just as they have a duty to treat us as full humans not raw data, we have a duty to view them as full humans, not bureaucratic symbols.

Communal justice refers to the form of justice we have between neighbors or citizens and is the most common form of justice. Your everyday activities are filled with actions which are either just or unjust. Either you are giving your neighbor his or her due, or you are unjustly withholding it.

The aim of communal justice is the stranger, not your loved one. Anyone can give their loved one what is due them, but what about the homeless person, your impossible-to-live-with neighbor, the undocumented aliens at your border, the person who has hurt you in the past? Justice demands that we impartially give each person what they are owed. In every interaction we have, we have an opportunity to do justice or withhold justice. Can we practice that justice even when it is inconvenient and uncomfortable, even when it doesn't fit the narrative we have for ourselves or our politics?

Perhaps the most challenging aspect of communal justice is that it always eludes us. Every action we take makes us a "debtor or a creditor,"[13] so that we are constantly owing each other something in the form of restitution. I owe you an apology. You owe me an answer. I owe you lunch. You owe me forgiveness. And so on, forever. We sin against each other constantly, and so we must constantly be repenting. Pieper says this striving toward equality of justice "cannot be arrested. It must, rather, be constantly, reestablished, 'restored anew.'"[14]

There is a reason Christ commanded us to forgive our neighbor "seventy-seven times" (Matthew 18:22). We're always in a state of reestablishing justice in a fallen world. We are all constantly in the process of restitution seeking, never arriving at total justice this side of paradise. And, Pieper warns, "Any claim to erect a definitive and unalterable order in the world must of necessity lead to something inhuman."[15] In other words, any government system or social justice movement that promises to create equality through some program is doomed not only to fail but to create a more inhuman condition, because disequilibrium is the natural state in a fallen world. This does *not* mean that we accept injustice. On the contrary, the just person recognizes that injustice and disorder are the natural state of things in the fallen world and does what is in his or her power to make restitution and bring justice. As we shall see in chapter six on hope, the constant striving toward justice Pieper is describing here is not a hopeless striving, but a hope*ful* one, based on Christ's ultimate justice.

One approach to seeking justice would be to calculate with an obsessive mind all the wrongs you've ever done and all the things you are owed so that you can perfect your justice as much as possible, but Pieper warns against this: "Communal life will necessarily become inhuman if man's dues to man are determined by pure calculation. That the just man give to another what is *not* due to him is particularly important since injustice is the prevailing condition in our world."[16] We have an obligation to strive for justice, even if that means exceeding what is strictly *due*, and even if it falls short, because injustice is the condition of the world. To prevent an inhuman world, we need to practice a justice that is driven by *grace* rather than *technique*. We need a *prodigal* justice.

THE LIMITS OF JUSTICE: WHY WE CAN'T GIVE EVERYONE THEIR DUE

Justice has limits. Knowing those limits allows us to appreciate our place in the world and the nature of our obligations. Our most fundamental relationship, which is between ourselves and God, is one where we cannot give the other person what they are due. We owe God an unrepayable debt. Typically we think of this debt in relation to the wages of sin. Christ paid our debt of sin on the cross once and for all. But *our existence itself is an infinite debt*. Insofar as being alive is of incalculable value and wonder, we owe the Creator and sustainer of our existence an infinite debt. Undoubtedly there are times when we are skeptical of the value of life, but objectively, being alive is miraculous, regardless of what struggles you face. Your ability to see, to taste, to touch, to smell, to hear is miraculous. The passing of time is miraculous. And there is nothing we can do to make ourselves worthy of the miracle of our being. We must receive it as a gift of grace from a loving God.

And so right off the bat, as soon as we are conceived, we owe God more than we can ever repay:

> *Before* any subsequent claim is made by men, indeed even before the mere possibility of such a human claim arises, comes the fact that man has been made a gift by God (of his being) such that his nature cannot ever "make it good," discharge it, "deserve" it, or return it again. Man can never say to God: We are even.[17]

One response to this debt is bitterness. If you think about someone who receives a precious gift they can never repay, you can see all the ways we react wrongly to God. We minimize the grandeur of the gift, "Oh, it's not that expensive." Or we deny that we wanted the gift in the first place, "I never even asked for this!" Or we imagine that we can pay back through our own gift giving, "After I give him this gift, we will be even." In one way or another, each of these responses denies the true nature of the gift of existence. As we will see in chapter six on hope as a virtue, this way of thinking is a form of hopelessness, of despair.

The challenge is to recognize the wonder of being alive and our inability to be worthy of existence by our efforts and yet receive it as a blessing. That takes courage.

I began describing our unrepayable debt to God because that debt is the easiest to see, once we accept the reality and consequences of our sins and the miracle of life itself. But there are many other debts we cannot pay back, and in these relationships, justice looks like a generous giving coupled with an acceptance of grace. The most significant of these relationships is to our parents or those who raised us.

Parenting is a stressful, confusing, and often thankless activity. Even the best parent doesn't really know what they are doing. They are stumbling around in the dark, hoping and praying that they don't mess up their children too badly. And the world places inhuman pressures on parents to be perfect. There is constant attention paid to the failings of parents and how poor parenting damages children.

The reality is that we all damage each other merely by living. Causing harm is an inescapable part of human life. All that we can sometimes do is choose what harm, or mitigate that harm, or apologize—which is no small part of the task of justice. Granted, there are parents who spurn their God-given obligation to their children, who neglect and abuse them. I do not claim such parents are owed an "unrepayable debt" of gratitude. I believe we honor such parents by holding them to the standards of their roles, which sometimes means setting firm boundaries and even seeking civil justice. When I say that we owe our parents a debt,

I'm referring to imperfect parents, certainly, but not abusive or negligent.

The debt we owe to such parents or guardians is immense. Not as immense as our debt to God, but still not something we can ever pay back. Living with our infinite debt to God is hard enough, but how do we justly owe an unrepayable debt to another person?

We begin by accepting their gift as a gift—not as a transaction. Our parents' care for us is an act of love which we respond to in kind, showing them honor and respect and care. As they cared for us in our young age, we ought to care for them, especially in their old ages. If Christians were to practice this, we would become known as the people who care for their elderly. We ought to have that label. People who care for their elderly.

In a more abstract way, we owe an unrepayable debt to our city, particularly if it is actually functioning as a proper city and providing us the care and nurture we discussed earlier. In a less immediate way than our parents, our city helps to raise us, contributes to our education, our safety, our health, our flourishing, and our spiritual well-being. We owe our city a debt for that nurture and care, no matter how flawed it was. And we can't calculate how we can pay it back by serving in the city for a number of years as a public school teacher, for example. We have to accept that debt as grace and seek to honor that city by serving it in return.

Because we can never meet the full demand of justice in this world, not only to God, our parents, our city, but even to each other, it is important that we strive to go beyond formal justice in any given situation: "[I]n order to keep the world going, we must be prepared to give what is not in the strictest sense obligatory."[18] Justice is necessary, but not sufficient for the world to function.

Specifically, Pieper argues that excessive giving is necessary for culture to be *human*. We need kindness, friendliness.[19] A culture that thinks only in terms of formal justice, what is *technically* due to each person, will cease to be human because it only thinks in terms of technicalities. Something more is needed to allow our culture to flourish.

You see examples of this in government bureaucrats who fulfill their duties, approving forms, let's say, but who fail to show basic courtesy and kindness. Or corporations who outsource customer service to phone farms which have insane wait times. Technically they are providing customer service, but there is no basic human kindness involved. Or customers who refuse to smile or show any human warmth because technically their only obligation is to pay for their product or service. You cannot demand a smile, but without smiles the world grows cold and inhuman. It is precisely *because* justice has a human limit that exceeding the formal limit of justice is necessary to make life human.

The posture of the Christian should be one of generosity, not just in giving money, but in time, in eye contact, in smiles, in gestures of kindness. Elsewhere in my writing I have referred to this posture as *prodigality* and argued that it is a powerful response to a culture of *technique* which seeks to maximize efficiency.[20] A strictly exacting practice of justice is one that focuses entirely on what can be measured and therefore performed more efficiently. A prodigal justice goes beyond what is strictly necessary.

We see a model for this prodigal justice in Jesus' teaching in the Sermon on the Mount in Matthew 5:40-41: "And if anyone would sue you and take your tunic, let him have your cloak as well. And if anyone forces you to go one mile, go with him two miles." Formal justice might demand so much of us, but grace calls us to something prodigal. The more our culture is driven by efficiency, the more exacting we will become. The less grace we will have for each other and the less basic human kindness. To cultivate a true, full habit of justice, you must not merely follow legal justice, you must also consider how to be just to your neighbor through your friendliness. The just person is a kind person, not the one who follows the letter of the law most correctly.

Ultimately in this life, we can't give everyone what they are due. We owe too many people too many things. But what we can do is work to make the world a more human space by acting with prodigal justice, offering up more than what is formally demanded of us, showing grace and kindness in every interaction we have, because our Father in heaven has shown us grace upon grace.

JUSTICE APPLIED

Charity. Perhaps the most challenging implication of justice is what we owe our neighbor in need. As evangelicals raised in a capitalist country, our default is to perceive charity as belonging *solely* in the category of love. After all, charity means love. Historically, Christians have understood charity as a duty, as something we owe our neighbor in need, which puts it in the category of justice as well as love.[21] This is not an issue of semantics either. If we view charity exclusively as an act of love and not justice, we may begin to view it as an add-on to our faith, as an optional activity for super-Christians, rather than a basic command for all of us. Our wealth does not belong to us; it belongs to God. And if it belongs to God, and he calls us to be charitable with our wealth (see 1 John 3:17 and Luke 12:33), then we owe our neighbors in need our wealth. This is a difficult teaching in a country where abundance is treated as a standard quality of the Good Life, but there it is.

What's remarkable to consider is how this country and the world would look different if evangelicals gave even when it hurt, instead of only giving out of abundance. Our tendency is still to believe that those who give the largest amounts are the ones most worthy of honor, when Christ clearly taught in Luke 21:1-4, the story of the widow's mite, that it is those who give out of their poverty, not their abundance, who give the most. Calvin writes, "Every one should rather consider, that however great he is, he owes himself to his neighbors, and that the only limit to his beneficence is the failure of his means. The extent of these should regulate that of his charity."[22] In other words, the greater wealth God has given you, the greater your obligation to give. The only thing that should hinder you from charity should be "failure of means," the inability to provide basic necessities for yourself. If we took God's commands to be charitable seriously, how much poverty could be alleviated? How much addiction could be alleviated? How much culture creation could we accomplish?

Unfortunately, most Americans don't feel like they can afford to give. Even as they move into the middle class and add yet another streaming service, they convince themselves that sponsoring a child overseas or helping in a homeless shelter or even tithing regularly is too demanding. There will always be an excuse not to give to the poor or to the church or to worthy institutions. Always. But if justice demands that you give, you have a duty to give. I cannot tell you how much to give—that's where prudence and, as we shall see later, temperance come to our aid. But I can say that justice says we owe the poor and needy our charity and we owe the church our tithe, and I would add that we owe our communal institutions financial support.

I think we need to be practicing three forms of charitable giving. First, we should support our local churches through tithes and offerings. We are commanded to tithe, and through our tithes we support the work of the local church as well as missionaries, diaconal work, and evangelism. Second, we should be giving directly to organizations that care for the most needy in the world, especially those closest to our homes. We should not exclusively deal with the poverty in our neighborhoods, but we should always start there. Begin with the needs in your own family and neighborhood and work outwards. This includes programs that address generational poverty, that build skills, and that improve educational standards so that people can earn a decent living. We can disagree on the *best* way to address poverty through charity, but we can't neglect the demands of charity.

And third, we should invest in culture-building institutions. By this I mean schools, colleges, institutes, publications, museums, art foundations, grant-awarding bodies, and the like. This is a practical way we can shore up the ruins of a decaying culture. It may feel like investing in culture is unimportant compared to the work of supporting the church and alleviating poverty, but a healthy culture leads to prosperity for all. Our souls need to be fed as well as our bellies.

If you doubt the value of supporting culture-building institutions, consider the growing mental health crisis in the United States. Whatever its causes and the possible solutions, they will involve holistic soul care: prayer and spiritual counseling, professional mental health assistance, as well as great works of art and cultural criticism that help explain and deal with the problems causing the mental health crisis. Or consider the current political crisis facing the United States. Without strong cultural institutions, we can't expect to have the educated and virtuous citizens necessary to guide a democracy toward justice.

Even while our culture tells us that we are our own and belong to ourselves, and that our only obligation is to look out for our own interest, communal justice demands that we give charitably regardless of our income.

Racism. The last decade has seen a rise and slight decline in public discourse about racism in the United States, one of the most besetting issues of justice in American life. The rise began with a series of shootings of unarmed Black people, particularly of Trayvon Martin on February 26, 2012, and escalated to the

2020 George Floyd riots and protests. Since then, America seems to have lost its appetite for discussing racism, and while there are certainly still conversations about race happening, public universities are busy closing their Diversity, Equity, and Inclusion departments, and Black Lives Matters protests are no longer receiving any coverage, if they are happening at all.

During the thirteen years since Martin's tragic death, important and necessary revelations have surfaced about racism in America. Lingering biases have been exposed. Historical massacres have been publicized. Statues have been removed. Abuses have been revealed. And most importantly, many White Americans were forced to reckon with the fact that racism did not end with Jim Crow. Far from it. At the same time, the discourse about race, particularly on social media, became utterly toxic. Accusations of racism flew left and right. People became paranoid about accidentally being perceived as racist. Some began to assume that every White person was unconsciously racist, as if racism were the White original sin.

Rather than resolve these tensions, Americans seem to have just moved on to the next cultural war, in this case being transgender rights and the 2024 election. How can the virtue of justice help us see the sin of racism in America more clearly?

Justice demands that we give each person what they are due, so some people have called for a "colorblind" justice that utterly ignores concepts of race, but I think that misses the mark for a number of reasons. First, as the last thirteen years showed us, it is likely that we have our own biases that have blinded us to real systemic, institutional, historic, or personal racism in our country. Recall that prudence (which is necessary for justice!) requires us to see reality clearly. So often those who believe they understand the plight of Black and Brown Americans do so from a posture of confidence in their own powers of perception rather than *humility* and a loving-to-know posture. Recognizing that different races experience life in America differently is a step toward recognizing biases.

Second, you may *wish* race to be irrelevant in the way you make judgments about an individual, but so long as that individual suffers because of racism regularly, race still matters. It's a critical part of their experience of the world which will affect what is *due to them*. Specifically, what is due is kindness, grace, and sensitivity, just like you would offer anyone who has been wrongfully mistreated. If you are in the position to correct that mistreatment, it is your obligation according to justice to do so. Pretending race doesn't exist prevents us from acknowledging the reality of continued racism.

Justice also demands that we don't misuse the concept of racism. Some antiracist advocates have an expansive view of racism that takes in all of reality, so that nearly *every* problem in America is a result of White Supremacy. The tragedy of this view is that by blaming almost everything on racism, it has distracted from the real, ongoing issues of racial injustice that exist in our nation. When everything is racism, people begin to feel that nothing is racism, that the word doesn't refer to anything *specific*. The more carefully and accurately we can use our terms, the more justice we can bring about.

Another aspect of justice and race is reckoning with the history of racism in America. We'd like to imagine that this history is in the distant past, but the truth is that there are still many people living today who suffered under segregation and Jim Crow. The past is not a foreign country. As William Faulkner said, "The past is never dead. It's not even past."[23] It's here, right now. I believe we owe those who came before us the responsibility to bear the burden of the past, to remember the past, and to do what we reasonably can to rectify the past.

In T. S. Eliot's "Choruses from 'The Rock'" he captures this sense of duty to the past when he writes, "Of all that was done in the past, you eat the fruit, either rotten or ripe."[24] This is a grim and yet blessed reality. As humans we reap the benefits and the burdens of those who came before us. We don't earn their good accomplishments (think of democracy and great works of literature and art) and we aren't to blame for their sins. But we still have to cope with the consequences of both! So how are we to respond to these consequences? Eliot writes, "And all that is ill you may repair if you walk together in humble repentance, expiating the sins of your fathers."[25] In other words, we have the burden of striving to "repair" the "ill" done by our forefathers by walking "together in humble repentance," which I think can take many forms. I think it can take the simple form of learning and remembering a tragic history, or it can take the more serious form of making amends for past wrongs. It depends on the situation and what is prudent, reasonable, and possible at the time.

But I will say, as Pieper reminds us, we must be willing to go beyond formal justice to make the world a human place. I sometimes worry that our imaginations are too small when it comes to addressing the crimes and sins of the past. There may be situations when going beyond what is strictly required of a nation from a legal perspective is necessary to "expiate the sins of your fathers." I take Eliot here to be using poetic license with the word "sins." I don't think he means that we humans can literally expiate the sins of our fathers before God. I do think he believes we can do the hard work of recovering some of what was lost because of the sins of our fathers. And that, it seems to me, is what justice demands of us: that we work to recover some of what was lost by the sins and errors of the previous generations. I don't know what that looks like in your community, but I do know that we all have a responsibility to figure it out in our local context.

Justice demands much of us, more than we can bear on our own. Our response to the burden of justice is twofold. First, we should seek a prodigal justice, giving more than is strictly due when we can and when it is appropriate to make the world a more human and tolerable place. Second, we trust in Christ's finished work on the cross, his redemptive work making all things new, knowing that he is the one bringing ultimate justice to this world, not us. All our efforts for justice will be renewed and fulfilled in light of his miraculous second coming. But we still strive for justice today, because that is what we are called to, as it says in Micah 6:8, "He has told you, O man, what is good; and what does the LORD require of you but to do justice, and to love kindness, and to walk humbly with your God?" The virtue of justice is the practice of getting up and giving your neighbor his or her due every moment despite the fact that you will fail at times. It requires courage, and it is to courage that we turn next.

3

SUFFERING STEADFASTLY

FORTITUDE, OR COURAGE, has always been a difficult virtue to practice because it requires vulnerability: "To be brave actually means to be able to suffer injury."[1] Few of us like to be vulnerable, but life demands a great deal of courage from us precisely because it is filled with a great deal of suffering. Although we can and should avoid unnecessary suffering, we cannot avoid all suffering. It is going to affect us one way or another. We begin life suffering, with the shock of being removed from the womb, and we end life in some form of suffering. In between, various shocks, surprises, wounds, traumas, scars, and difficulties face us. As Christians, we are promised persecution as a particular form of suffering (2 Timothy 3:12). And so, the question becomes: How can we suffer well? How can we endure the suffering that we are going to face inevitably?

This is not a theoretical question, but a present, immediate, moment-by-moment question that we each have to face. The question of what makes life worth living can seem morbid but has a real, day-to-day reality to it. The person who hasn't answered the question of what makes life worth living is at risk of losing that life when things get difficult, and they will get difficult. Whether it comes in the form of complex trauma, acute tragedy, routine stress, or chronic illness (physical or mental), you will suffer in this life. And when that suffering seems to have no end, or when the suffering outweighs the joy you experience in life, it may feel irrational to continue living. So, among other ways of dealing with suffering (medical treatments, resolving conflicts, mental health services, and so on), we must develop the virtue of fortitude to endure suffering when it inevitably comes.

Mental health is one of the more common ways people have to deal with daily suffering in America today. According to the CDC, one in five adults lives with a mental health condition and one in eighteen lives with a *serious* mental health condition.[2] Nearly 29 percent of adults have been diagnosed with depression at some point in their lives.[3] The work done by scholar Alain Ehrenberg has shown that contemporary manifestations of depression tend to appear as inhibition and feelings of inadequacy, which are opposed to the virtue of fortitude.[4] The modern daily experience of life is often one of deep sorrow and a feeling of helplessness before a crushing and indifferent cosmos. No wonder it's difficult to have courage.

What makes fortitude particularly challenging in the contemporary world is that nearly every social force is oriented toward *reducing* our suffering and *removing* barriers to our goals at all costs. Inevitably, barriers and suffering still exist, but it is remarkable that so many corporations and governments and other organizations are devoted to offering us goods and services that simplify our lives. The drive for efficiency is called *technique*, and sociologist Jacques Ellul, in his book *The Technological Society*, says that technique defines our modern world, with the promise that all paths lead to less suffering, less difficulty, and fewer challenges.[5] We either have the cure for whatever troubles us or we are working on developing the cure. It may cost you more than you can afford, but the point is that all physical, mental, spiritual, commercial, legal, and social problems have or will shortly have a solution available for the right price.

Meanwhile, the reality is that life is hard. Physical and sexual abuse, trauma, mental illness, spiritual depressions, and the chaos of everyday life make it hard to keep going sometimes regardless of all the world's *techniques* to fix everything. A result of this is that you feel like a failure for continuing to struggle. You feel like *you* are the problem.

This promise that life is getting easier and easier is one reason why I think some social critics, like social psychologist Jonathan Haidt, have begun to worry that younger people are no longer *resilient* enough.[6] Adults have conditioned young people to think that difficulties and hardships are *always* problems to be solved rather than normal parts of the human experience that we sometimes must simply endure with grace. So students are unprepared to face challenging math problems. Or they shut down when they experience tense, high-stakes social situations. Or they give up on a sport or musical instrument after they make a mistake or fail to perform up to society's standards. This could be any of us, really, not just young people. Plenty of older people seem incapable of coping with the shocks of life. And that's not a criticism of anyone. It's difficult for us to develop the virtue of fortitude when it seems like there is always a technique for us to use to overcome suffering. Our entire system is designed to *prevent* the development of fortitude. Once again, we've been given "A heap of broken images."[7]

But we still use language of "courage" in our society, it's just that instead of referring to the courage of enduring suffering, we primarily use it to refer to those who choose to *live authentically*. When I look inside myself, discover or create my identity, and live authentically to that identity regardless of society's values, views, or opinions, I am living the courageous life of the individual. This is what some philosophers and sociologists would call "expressive individualism," and it's one of the defining social frameworks of our age.[8]

In many ways, the modern hero's journey is the story of freeing oneself from the strictures of the community into radical autonomous authenticity. And of course, to stand apart from the community takes courage. Today we see this primarily done on social media, where people can carefully cultivate images of themselves to project out into the world, and the primary ways people seem to be finding authenticity is in their gender or sexuality. But there are many manifestations of this, including by trying to look and act "authentically" Christian according to some cultural, extrabiblical standard. Anytime someone seeks to break with societal norms to live authentically to their self-chosen inner identity, regardless of their political leanings, they are practicing expressive individualism. And in our culture, that is the epitome of courage.

The problem with this understanding of courage is not that it doesn't take courage to challenge societal norms; it's that it is an impoverished image of fortitude. It assumes that the only honorable form of suffering is suffering for authenticity, when, as we shall see, there are millions of honorable reasons to suffer in life. Because true fortitude is about suffering *for the sake of the good*. Authenticity is just one of many goods in life, and sometimes it is not even that. Sometimes "authenticity" is only a story we tell ourselves to justify the pursuit of a lifestyle we hope will give us fulfillment.

Fortitude is difficult to cultivate in contemporary society because we are trained to believe it is unnecessary, except when it comes to asserting our independence from society.

FORTITUDE DEFINED

Right before Christ was betrayed by Judas, he went up to the Mount of Olives with his disciples to pray, and in this prayer we received the most powerful depiction of fortitude in human history:

> And he withdrew from them about a stone's throw, and knelt down and prayed, saying, "Father, if you are willing, remove this cup from me. Nevertheless, not my will, but yours be done." And there appeared to him an angel from heaven, strengthening him. And being in agony he prayed more earnestly; and his sweat became like great drops of blood falling down to the ground. And when he rose from prayer, he came to the disciples and found them sleeping for sorrow, and he said to them, "Why are you sleeping? Rise and pray that you may not enter into temptation." (Luke 22:41-46)

At this moment, Christ knew he was about to enter into tremendous suffering to take on the sins of the world, to be beaten, humiliated, and killed on our behalf. And quite humanly, a part of Christ was hesitant to walk through this suffering, so he prayed that God the Father would remove the cup of suffering from him. And yet he recognized the good and was willing to suffer incomprehensible pain for that good. The good was (and always is) God's will. Accepting God's will was not easy, however; Christ sweat like drops of blood. But eventually he rose from his prayer, confident in what he had to do, and chastised the disciples for sleeping. This is fortitude.

A simple definition of fortitude is perseverance under suffering for the sake of a greater good. From this definition follows a few conclusions. First, we must allow ourselves to be vulnerable in this life: "Fortitude presupposes vulnerability; without vulnerability there is no possibility of fortitude."[9] Christ made himself vulnerable by becoming human in the incarnation, and the fulfillment of that vulnerability was his death on the cross in obedience to God. In the above prayer, we see his human vulnerability on full display. Likewise, we should accept our own vulnerability in obedience to God. I'm not recommending recklessness, but we should avoid the safetyism that keeps us from all forms of vulnerability. To be human is to be vulnerable, and to be vulnerable is to be capable of the virtue of fortitude, which is an honorable thing.

Second, fortitude involves suffering, and the ultimate form of suffering is death: "[M]artyrdom is the essential root of all Christian fortitude."[10] Most of us in the modern West will not face the threat of death for our faith, although we will be required to endure lesser forms of persecution, whether that comes as loss of career opportunities, loss of popularity, or even loss of political rights. In a lesser but still meaningful way, taking up our cross daily for Christ in the practice of fortitude is a minor kind of martyrdom (Luke 9:23). We die to ourselves daily for Christ. In that sense, the life of the Christ *is* the life of the martyr, which takes nothing away from the sacrifice paid by martyrs who have died for the faith today or in history, but it does give us a model for how to live—sacrificially.

Third, fortitude is never done for its own sake but for a greater good: "The brave man suffers injury not for its own sake, but rather as a means to preserve or to acquire a deeper, more essential intactness."[11] This is an important point since some people have a perverse tendency to romanticize suffering and turn it into a sign of their holiness or, in this case, courage. But the purpose of bravery is to accomplish something greater. To protect someone. To preserve something good. For the sake of your faith, your life, your family, your country, or the stranger in need.

There is a reason fortitude comes after prudence and justice in our list of virtues, for without prudence and justice, you cannot be properly brave. We tend to have a hypermasculine, rash, adrenaline-fueled vision of what courage looks like, but the virtue of fortitude avoids rash decisions. Fortitude requires us to suffer for the sake of the good, but first we have to know what that good is. And that knowledge requires the virtues of prudence and justice: "[O]nly he who is just and prudent can also be brave; to be really brave is quite impossible without at the same time being prudent and just also."[12]

Prudence and justice lead us to reflect on what the good ultimately is before we go risking our lives, our physical health, our mental health, our time, our money, our social capital, and so on for a cause. Society calls us to act *now* on every social issue that comes up, to have an opinion and make our voices heard "courageously." But prudence requires us to weigh the costs, to examine if this is truly a *good* cause worth suffering for. Because again, not all suffering is courageous. Enduring needless suffering is not courageous, it's just foolish: "Without the 'just cause' there is no fortitude."[13] Christ did not suffer needlessly on the cross. He suffered with a purpose. So should we be courageous.

Courage is not the absence of fear, but rather the willingness to endure despite fear.[14] For Pieper, fear is a necessary aspect of true fortitude. It is only when all else fails and we are face-to-face with our fear and we choose to endure anyway for the sake of God that we are truly brave. So often we view fear as a hinderance to acting courageously, when it is precisely the person who is afraid who can act courageously!

Fortitude is divided into two main parts by Thomas Aquinas: attack and endurance.[15] And each has its place. Attack is when we see an evil being done and we have the power to stop that evil and we risk or incur injury for the greater good. There will be many times in our lives when we will be called to this kind of courage, times when we need to speak up when someone is sexually harassing a colleague or using a racial slur, times when we need to stand up for the unborn or the elderly or the widow or the orphan. Some of us will be called to act with courage in war or as first responders. These moments require strength of character, a firm grasp of what is just, and a willingness to suffer for others.

But Aquinas and Pieper argue that the greater part of fortitude is endurance. Because for most of us, our daily experience of fortitude will be one of long-suffering: "[F]ortitude primarily and ultimately proves its genuine character" through endurance, when to "endure is objectively the only remaining possibility of resistance."[16] And often in life, enduring suffering is the only remaining possibility of resistance. There are many thorns in the flesh that we must simply endure. There are many injustices that we must wait for God to set right. There are many tears that only God can dry. And so we must endure and carry on. We move through our lives despite the suffering.

But is this endurance merely quietism or passivity? Shouldn't fortitude be more muscular and active? Can courage really be so quiet? The answer to these objections is that enduring suffering is not passive at all, but an *active stance*, not for the timid or resentful, but for the courageous who put their hope in God's ultimate justice. When the psalmist cries out for help from God, continuing to hope in God's deliverance but having no immediate means of resistance against overwhelming enemies, that is courage (Psalm 69). When Paul endures the thorn in his flesh, that is courage (2 Corinthians 12:7). And when you get out of bed each morning despite the suffering you may face, that is courage.

We tend to think of courage as a virtue for warriors, and it certainly is, but we do ourselves an injustice if we do not see it as a basic virtue for all humans. We are all called by design to display the virtue of fortitude in our lives, sometimes in attacks against evil or for the good, and sometimes patient endurance of suffering for the good, but in all things we suffer for God's glory, not for the sake of suffering or for our own glory.

It is a hard saying but true that all the best things in this life involve pain, suffering, sacrifice, and great risk, and therefore, fortitude. Marriage, children, friendship, art, and health all require you to sacrifice part of your life for some greater good. They each involve the risk of heartbreak. They entail personal suffering and the pain of personal growth. They involve physical and mental pain. But they also are sources of great joy and personal satisfaction and meaning. Great art has the power to break your heart to regrow it into something more beautiful, good, and true. But the breaking still hurts, despite the outcome.

If you are too cowardly to read beautiful books that challenge your perspective, you will never have the joy of maturing aesthetically. If you are too cowardly to talk to someone, you'll never have the joy of a relationship with them, even though you do risk rejection and betrayal. If you don't have the fortitude to have children, you miss the wonder of caring for the growth of another human. "All things of grace and beauty such that one holds them to one's heart have a common provenance in pain," wrote Cormac McCarthy.[17] And he's right. Even your spiritual walk requires great fortitude. To endure the process of sanctification requires you to endure self-denial and suffering. What is saying "no" to your sins but a form of suffering, even if it is suffering for your own good? And so, to live a good life, one honoring to God, involves the development of the virtue of fortitude.

FORTITUDE APPLIED

Daily suffering. The true test of fortitude is our ability to patiently endure suffering for the good. It is the monotony of suffering that gets to you in the end, the knowledge that you will go to bed suffering and wake up to more suffering, having to live this same day over again with all its mundane indignities. Fortitude teaches you the importance of enduring great suffering as a normal part of human life for the goodness of all those around you. Fortitude is a million tiny decisions to keep going, to rise out of bed, to take a step to the block, to live and move and have your being despite great suffering.

Fortitude can look like enduring the monotony of daily housework without plunging into self-pity or despair. It can look like going days, weeks, or months without feeling peace or joy because of life's daily struggles or a mental illness. Fortitude means carrying on even when you feel like giving up. And it's a powerful witness to those around us. When your children or friends or coworkers see you being resilient in the face of hardship, it gives them the imaginal space to be resilient too. As humans, we can only act on what we know to be possible, and so if every example you have is of someone who folds under pressure, you will only ever imagine yourself folding under pressure. But if you have models of resilience, then you can imagine yourself as resilient.

You may not have any models of resilience in your life. It could be that everyone you know merely complains, gives up, shifts blame, or has excuses when they struggle. But you can be that model of resilience for others. You can be the one example of fortitude that many people see, and that counts for something. To be a model of resilience like this does not mean cultivating a certain kind of image, which is only another form of expressive individualism. Instead, it involves an unassuming simplicity of focus on what is good regardless of feelings. And it *allows* others to witness that focus on the good in action in your life.

Recall that the ideal form of fortitude is martyrdom. While most of us in the United States won't be martyred for our faith, we may experience some persecution, and all of us are asked to die to ourselves daily (Luke 9:23). When such times come, what will be asked of us is to bear with our suffering without losing hope. The source of our strength is Christ in God, and the example of fortitude is Christ's suffering in the Garden of Gethsemane the night before his crucifixion. As Christ shows us, it is appropriate for us to plead with God for a different outcome. We can desire that God's will be done but still beg God to use a different path to that will than the one we fear. But we must be ready to accept that we may need to sweat like drops of blood in agony. Yet still God is good.

The passion reminds us that even when life feels unbearably hard, God is faithful and is working all things together for good. It should be a great comfort to us that we serve a God who faced suffering even though he desired not to suffer death. He understands what it feels like to desire God's will while desiring relief from suffering. He understands what it feels like for the Father to seem to turn his face away, to be abandoned, although he could never truly be abandoned by his Father because of the nature of the Trinity. And neither can we be truly abandoned because the Holy Spirit lives in us.

In a lesser but still instructive way, choosing to live each day despite the reality of suffering is paradoxically a form of martyrdom, of dying to self. The choice to live is the choice to suffer for the sake of honoring God. We honor God by living out the life he has given us even when it hurts. We die to self when we allow ourselves to endure pain and heartache for the sake of loving our neighbor—which is precisely what God asks of us. There may come times in your life when rising out of bed feels impossible. When you can't imagine being physically, let alone mentally and emotionally, present to your family or friends. And in those moments, the act of rising out of bed and going to your family or friends and being with them is a sacrifice of love. It honors God by enacting his creation (you!) and it loves your family or friends. This requires great courage.

We don't acknowledge this enough, but day-to-day life demands a great deal of courage, courage which will inevitably be tested. Our task is to be faithful to the life God has granted us. We must recognize the good of life and persevere through the daily indignities and travails that come our way for that good.

Romantic relationships. A rising percentage of people are not getting married in the United States.[18] This rate has bounced back a bit from a Covid low, but it's still quite low from a historic perspective.[19] In my experience working with young people, there is usually a great desire to get married, but finding the right person and taking the time to develop a relationship with them can be barriers to marriage. Realistically, the older one gets without getting married, the harder it gets to find a spouse and adjust to married life. I wish this were not the case, but in my experience it is. So the pressure to find a spouse and partner up can be overwhelming. So overwhelming, in fact, that it requires *courage* to pursue a relationship at whatever stage of life you are at.

Anything good and beautiful in this life requires courage and sacrifice to obtain, and a spouse is no exception. Courage begins with the commitment to find a spouse, the confidence that you are a worthy marriage partner for someone, and the humility to grow spiritually, mentally, physically, and emotionally in whatever ways necessary to become that partner. This includes taking an honest assessment of yourself to see where you need to prayerfully mature before seeking a relationship. Are there besetting sins in your life that would be harmful to a relationship? Are you trustworthy and disciplined? Do you have reasonable goals for yourself? If you can't give a good answer to these questions, then have the courage to *become* the kind of person who *can,* with the help of the Holy Spirit and a local community of support. You can grow. Don't give in to despair. Have hope and courage and seek to become an honorable, desirable potential spouse.

When you see someone who you think you might want to get to know better as a potential spouse, or even a friend, fortitude demands that you risk injury to your pride and walk over and introduce yourself. Of course you will be afraid, but again, courage involves fear by its very nature. And you may in fact be injured. You may be ignored or rejected. That is fine. That is their right. But your task is to be brave enough to put yourself in danger of suffering for the sake of the greater good, in this case marriage. If you have been declined or rejected by someone, simply brush yourself off and carry on. Fortitude allows you to endure that suffering of rejection without wallowing in self-pity or indulging in selfish resentment. But you must take the risk for the good.

As C. S. Lewis has written, this risk is an essential part of love itself:

> There is no safe investment. To love at all is to be vulnerable. Love anything and your heart will certainly be wrung and possibly be broken. If you want to make sure of keeping it intact, you must give your heart to no one, not even to an animal. Wrap it carefully round with hobbies and little luxuries; avoid all entanglements; lock it up safe in the casket or coffin of your selfishness. But in that casket—safe, dark, motionless, airless—it will change. It will not be broken; it will become unbreakable, impenetrable, irredeemable. The alternative to tragedy, or at least to the risk of tragedy, is damnation. The only place outside Heaven where you can be perfectly safe from all the dangers and perturbations of love is Hell.[20]

Love requires courage, whether that love is love of a pet, a friend, or a spouse. If you desire marriage as a good, you must have courage to risk a broken heart to reach that good.

After you have begun a friendship, it is not enough to stay friends if you believe the person to be someone you have romantic feelings toward and would like to marry. If they are not already in a committed relationship, you must make yourself vulnerable, take the risk of injury, and confess your feelings. Maybe they will reciprocate, maybe they will deny you, maybe they will embarrass you. Who knows? But fortitude requires you to try. While there is time for prudence, to carefully consider someone's personality and faith commitments and possible fit as a spouse, there is no time for timidity—the endless debating over someone's qualities so that you never make the decision to act. If you have prudently judged that they are a good potential spouse, tell them how you feel. Offer to commit to a relationship. Explore the possibility of marriage further.

In addition, when weighing someone's qualities, you must be wary of the danger of FOMO, the fear of missing out, creeping in and making you timid. FOMO will tell you that as beautiful as she is, there might be someone more lovely who you'll be missing out on if you pursue her. FOMO will tell you that her laugh is annoying. FOMO will tell you that you *must* marry someone who plans to homeschool. FOMO will tell you that you *must* marry someone who shares your exact political views. The fear of missing out is a rigid, unrealistic standard for marriage that will likely leave you lonely. Marriage involves compromise and commitment and learning to love someone's unique being in the world, not who you imagine they *must* be. FOMO will make you timid because you'll always imagine that around the corner is a better option, the One Right option, when right in front of you is a perfectly good, God-honoring person waiting to be pursued.

One of the most dangerous ideas our world has taught us is that since we only have one life to live, we must choose the one right spouse, the one right college major, the one right career, etc. In reality, God gives us many wise choices in this life, and it is our task to use the virtue of prudence with prayer to make a wise decision and rest in his grace. This is true for marriage.

Ultimately, if you desire the good of marriage, then you must have the courage to pursue that good. That includes working on yourself to prepare to become someone who is ready to be a spouse (spiritually, mentally, and physically), and taking the initiative to speak to people who you see as a potential spouse. It also requires the courage and hope (we'll talk about that soon!) to endure rejection and disappointment without turning to despair or bitterness. I don't know God's specific will for your life regarding marriage, but I do know that if you love him, he is actively working all things together for your good. Trust him and have courage.

Magnanimity. Aristotle taught that the virtue of magnanimity (which I am placing under the virtue of fortitude for reasons that will become clear) was a largeness of spirit.[21] One who is magnanimous is capable of great things and does those great things.[22] There is some question about whether Christians can be magnanimous, since for Aristotle it had to do with a kind of pridefulness and a sense of superiority over "lesser" people. But I want to offer a reclaiming of the concept for our own time. Perhaps it might offend some more traditionalists, but I think the virtue has much to teach us, if we alter it slightly.

To understand magnanimity, it's helpful to look at its opposite, pusillanimity, or timidity. People who are pusillanimous may be capable of great things but fail to act on their talents. Like in Christ's parable of the talents, this person hides their talents in the earth and hopes that's good enough for God (Matthew 25:14-30). They don't have the courage to *risk* anything.

Aristotle describes the condition this way:

> For the pusillanimous person is worthy of goods, but deprives himself of the goods he is worthy of, and would seem to have something bad in him because he does not think

> he is worthy of the goods. Indeed he would seem not to know himself; for if he did, he would aim at the things he is worthy of, since they are good.[23]

To be pusillanimous is to be afraid to be worthy of good things, to be afraid to apply for a job you are qualified for because you don't *feel* like you are worthy. This is why, with Aquinas, I believe it's helpful to think of magnanimity as under fortitude, because to be magnanimous, as we shall see, is to act courageously with the talents God has given you.

Many people today feel conflicted about *ambition*. Young women are encouraged to be ambitious and follow their dreams, and yet when they do so they are often viewed as "bossy" or "aggressive." Young men are sometimes viewed as too masculine or hostile if they follow their ambitions in their careers. Yet we also shame them if they don't achieve enough with their lives. These mixed signals lead to anxiety and confusion, understandably. There are reasons for these mixed signals, we should acknowledge. Untempered ambition can be a very ugly thing. It hurts other people, ruins personal relationships, damages your health, and leaves you empty. And yet, ambition itself is not entirely bad. The desire to achieve great things can *lead* to great things. Without that desire, without the courage to attempt greatness, it will never happen. So what we need is a model for ambition that is righteous. One that does not lead us into self-centered, sinful pride, but is also not timid. I think one answer to that is magnanimity.

As I would like to use the term, to be *magnanimous* is to have the courage to use the talents and gifts God has given you to their fullest extent to his glory and to the edification of your neighbor. This involves taking risks, whether that be submitting poems for publication even though you are afraid they are no good, or applying to a prestigious school even though you feel unqualified, or starting a company even though you are afraid it may fail, or volunteering to lead a project at work that might lead to a promotion. As with all examples of fortitude, you see the greater good and you pursue it by taking on the risk.

But with magnanimity you are specifically applying this to your talents to achieve a kind of greatness that glorifies God and blesses your neighbor. By "greatness" I have in mind an excellence in whatever you put your hand to, so this applies equally to the work of a plumber as to the work of a world-famous painter. For Aristotle magnanimity was a virtue for few, elect individuals. I believe that if we understand magnanimity to be the pursuit of the greatness God has created us to pursue, whatever that greatness might be, even the greatness of a quiet life of excellence, then it is a virtue for all people. And it takes a great deal of courage.

According to Aristotle's understanding of magnanimity, it's impossible to be magnanimous without acquiring the other virtues as well. In other words, to be truly worthy of great things, you cannot be a ruthless "ladder climber"; you need to be a person of character and integrity, a person of virtue.[24] I think Aristotle is mostly right. A magnanimous person ought to be a virtuous person. I would only add that our worthiness to pursue a great venture is not only based on our achievements, abilities, and qualifications, but on our union with Christ. Because we are united with Christ, we are worthy to pursue the greatness he has created us for, whatever that may be in our lives.

Ambition, understood through the lens of magnanimity, is not something to be ashamed of, but honored. It is a way of exercising God's creation—you! But it does require courage, the courage to fully embody who God created you to be.

No one wants to be timid, but everyone wants a life of ease. To be courageous requires us to forgo a life of ease, which was never really an option to begin with, and accept that suffering is a basic part of life. When we endure that suffering for God's glory, then we are practicing the virtue of fortitude. While you may think of courage as a virtue only for warriors, it turns out to be a basic virtue of life. Through the forces of *technique*, our society will invite us to ignore fortitude and cope with life through other means: chemical, technological, entertainment, sexual, and so on. But none of these will prepare us for the challenge of living. Only the practice of fortitude, which reminds us that we bear these sufferings for God's glory, can do that.

4

LIVING MODERATELY

OURS IS AN AGE OF INTEMPERANCE, an age of disorder and disharmony of the self. Nowhere is this more evident than in the prevalence of addiction. The French sociologist Alain Ehrenberg has argued, "Depression and addiction are the two sides of the sovereign individual, the person who believes herself to be the author of her own life."[1] This idea of belonging to yourself or being a "sovereign individual" is the prevailing societal ideology of our time. And Ehrenberg seems to be correct that depression is a natural outcome of that ideology. In 2023, a Gallup poll revealed the percentage of adults having been diagnosed with depression during their lifetime had reached a new record high.[2] We are a depressed people, and arguably part of that depression comes from the unbearable burden of being responsible for our own existence in the world. But what's interesting is his other observation: that addiction is the other side of the sovereign individual. And sure enough, we are addicted. We're addicted to almost everything: TV, smartphones, sex, gambling, caffeine, sugar, TikTok, Instagram, the news, alcohol, pornography, cannabis. Our engagement patterns with the world are deeply disordered toward addiction and intemperate habits.

According to the National Institutes of Health, "40.3 million people in the United States had an [substance use disorder] in

2020."[3] In a country of 333 million, that is a significant percentage of Americans struggling with addictions to things like alcohol, opioids, tobacco, and cannabis. But such addictions are nothing new. What is new is smartphone addiction, with nearly 57 percent of users self-reporting that they are addicted to their phones.[4]

Another new development has been the explosion of sports gambling, with a 2018 Supreme Court case that allowed states to legalize the practice. Currently, "The National Council on Problem Gambling estimates that approximately 2.5 million adults in the U.S. are severely addicted to gambling, and another four to six million people have mild to moderate gambling problems."[5] While we don't yet have data on how much sports gambling has increased overall gambling addictions, there are reports of gambling addiction call centers being inundated with calls since legalization.[6] One study found an increase in bankruptcy filings in states which allowed sports gambling.[7] Which makes sense, because the ubiquity of advertising and the ability to gamble anytime anywhere on your smartphone has made gambling much more attractive, particularly to young men.

Another new development has been the explosion of pornography with the internet, and with that explosion has come addiction. Among mental health professionals there is some debate about whether pornography addiction is a "real thing," but "roughly 11% of men and 3% of women reported some agreement with the statement 'I am addicted to pornography.'"[8] Finally, one study found that of video game users of the platform Steam, "between 14.6% and 18.3% of the users on this platform can be considered addicted."[9]

We almost all seem to be addicted to something, and a major reason for that is that there are strong forces working to get us addicted. Video games are designed to be addictive. Smartphones and social media are designed to be addictive. Sports gambling is designed to be addictive, despite the cute little help line they include in advertisements in case you "have a gambling problem." There are many people in the world who devote their lives to getting you addicted to substances and devices which are destructive to your soul (what a terrible way to make a living). There are many reasons why someone falls into addiction, so I don't want to minimize the struggle to get out of addiction, and if you find yourself addicted to things like alcohol, gambling, or sex, please seek professional help. But at the societal level, our collective tendency toward addiction betrays a failure of inner order, a failure to exercise the virtue of temperance.

It is exceedingly difficult to live a temperate life in a society that demands you consume more than you need, you deserve whatever your eyes desire, and your addictions are just quirky forms of self-care. In many ways our economy depends on our intemperate living. If we all lived within our means and gave generously to those in need instead of indulging ourselves, what would happen to our consumer economy? We are encouraged to eat more, spend more, watch another episode, watch another Reel, and look lustfully at that woman all because we *deserve* it. We are the sovereign individual.

There is a *moral* weight to fulfilling our every desire. Because I belong to myself, it is morally imperative that I follow my desires because no one else can make me happy, which means that rightly ordering my inner life and behaviors toward some external standard of morality is a foreign concept. It doesn't make sense. Why would I choose to deny my happiness for someone else's values? Charles Taylor puts it this way, "For many people today, to set aside their own path in order to conform to some external authority just doesn't seem comprehensible as a form of spiritual life."[10] Instead, the moral pressure is to follow our hearts.

To indulge our desires. To order our behaviors according to what we love. It's another "heap of broken images."[11]

Alternatively, we may tend the opposite direction. We may deny ourselves reasonable, healthy, good things out of a vain effort to purify ourselves or feel good enough for the gaze of the opposite sex or society. Or we might perceive ourselves as unworthy of good things, and so we deny ourselves pleasures that God has deemed good out of self-punishment and self-loathing. Some people use self-denial as a means to achieve greater success, as a means of optimizing their lives so they can compete better in their careers or in the sexual competition. While there is nothing inherently wrong with living an optimized life, it can easily exchange your humanity for material success. As we shall see, intemperance doesn't only involve overindulgence, it also involves the failure to properly enjoy the good gifts God has given us.

TEMPERANCE DEFINED

As Jesus began his ministry of healing and teaching, and word of him spread, he did not pursue this fame but instead grounded himself with prayer and solitude: "But now even more the report about him went abroad, and great crowds gathered to hear him and to be healed of their infirmities. But he would withdraw to desolate places and pray" (Luke 5:15-16). From a human perspective, it's easy to imagine how tempting it would have been for Jesus to give in to the pursuit of power and fame. The people desired him and his attention. He could have given himself totally over to the quest for more attention and more praise, increasing his followers and honor. But Jesus practiced temperance. He knew his own limits and the purpose of his incarnation, and so he made sure to set aside time regularly to go off and pray. Notice that Luke contrasts the crowds with Jesus' withdrawing to pray. I think the prayers helped to reorient Christ to his mission and away from the buzz and excitement of the crowd. He ordered his inner life toward what was good. This is the virtue of temperance.

Temperance is typically associated with the idea of moderation, and sometimes moderation is involved in the virtue, but with a little reflection you can see why mere moderation is an inadequate definition. Moderation is a useful concept when you are talking about dessert portions, but what about murders or pornography? What is the virtuously moderate portion of pornography? None! So, we need a richer concept than moderation to understand what the virtue of temperance means, and Pieper helps us with that concept. He defines temperance as the act "to dispose various parts into one unified and ordered whole."[12] That's a bit abstract, but the key to understanding it is this concept of *order*.

A person is made up of various parts, various desires, impulses, intentions, memories, anxieties, fears, hopes, beliefs, commitments, passions, etc. We get a sense of this in Romans 7:15-25 when Paul talks about his struggles with the flesh:

> For I do not understand my own actions. For I do not do what I want, but I do the very thing I hate. Now if I do what I do not want, I agree with the law, that it is good. So now it is no longer I who do it, but sin that dwells within me. For I know that nothing good dwells in me, that is, in my flesh. For I have the desire to do what is right, but not the ability to carry it out. For I do not do the good I want, but the evil I do not want is what I keep on doing. Now if I do what I do not want, it is no longer I who do it, but sin that dwells within me. So I find it to be a law that when I want to do right, evil lies close at hand. For I delight in the law of God, in my inner being, but I see in my members another law waging war against the law of my mind and making me captive to the law of sin that dwells in my members. Wretched man

> that I am! Who will deliver me from this body of death? Thanks be to God through Jesus Christ our Lord! So then, I myself serve the law of God with my mind, but with my flesh I serve the law of sin.

Paul sees his members waging war against the law of his mind, and his conclusion is that it is only through Christ and a commitment to "serve the law of God with [his] mind" (temperance) that he can resist the law of sin in his flesh. The point here is that the natural state of humanity is that we are disordered internally. Our passions are at war with our reason. Like Paul, we often know the right thing to do but choose to follow our fleshly passions anyway, especially when the world tells us that we have a moral responsibility to follow those passions. Temperance is about ordering those desires so that they reflect God's will.

Another way of looking at the goal of temperance is for serenity of spirit:

> What is meant is the serenity that fills the inmost recesses of the human being, and is the seal and fruit of order. The purpose and goal of *temperantia* is man's inner order, from which alone this "serenity of spirit" can flow forth. "Temperance" signifies the realizing of this order within oneself.[13]

I'm not convinced that any of us can achieve this serenity this side of paradise, but I do believe it is a goal worth striving toward. The idea is to so carefully order your inner life that you are not angered or frustrated at petty things, you're not drawn into lustful thoughts, you're not tempted to lose control of yourself and scroll endlessly on your phone, and so on.

The virtue of temperance is ultimately the fruit of the Spirit of self-control listed in Galatians 5:23. I think we don't often take this fruit of the Spirit seriously enough as something to be striven after. And so when we read lists like the one I just gave, our reaction is to say, "Well, no one can do that." Rather than to say, "Lord, give me the self-control to turn from anger, lustful thoughts, and idleness with my phone." Self-control seems somehow too difficult to try, so we don't try it, which is why we need to reclaim the virtue of temperance (which again is just self-control by another name) and put in the hard work to move toward serenity.

One critical aspect of temperance that might make us uncomfortable is that it requires a turn inward toward ourselves: "Temperance implies that man should look to himself and his condition, that his vision and his will should be focused on himself."[14] On the surface this might seem selfish, self-centered, or self-absorbed, and indeed, Pieper warns that there is a dangerous version of this inward look.[15] You can focus on yourself and your desires in such a way as to become self-absorbed and fixated on your own inner life at the exclusion of others, but you can also practice healthy introspection.

The difference in part has to do with how much time and attention you place on yourself, but it also has to do with the *purpose* of your introspection. Are you examining yourself to check your intentions or evaluate your inner thought life for lustful or discriminatory thoughts about others? Or are you wallowing in self-accusations and doubts? The latter is like the worldly grief that does not produce repentance but only death mentioned by Paul in 2 Corinthians 7:10. The former can be life-giving and lead to repentance and an ordered mind.

The key to temperance is what Pieper calls "selfless self-preservation," whereas "Intemperance is self-destruction through the selfish degradation of the powers which aim at self-preservation."[16] In other words, temperance is focused on preserving yourself for the glory of God (which includes delighting in the existence he has given you!) and the good of your neighbor. Intemperance destroys the individual by taking the tools for self-preservation (sex, food, leisure, etc.) and degrading them. Selfless self-preservation is a beautiful way of reassessing the way we think of ourselves.

Often Christians err either on the side of selfishly giving in to their desires like the rest of the world, or they deny themselves out of a false sense of selflessness. Pieper's concept shows us another way. Preserving ourselves is actually *selfless* when it rightly orders the gifts of preservation God has given us. For example, sex with your spouse is actually a selfless good when it is done in the context of marriage between a man and a woman. Eating a delicious meal is selfless self-preservation so that you can care for those around you. As we saw, Jesus practiced selfless self-preservation by going off to pray in desolate places.

Meanwhile, overeating so that you cannot help others because you are napping on the couch or undereating so that you are hangry are not examples of selfless self-preservation. You owe it to God, others, and yourself to defend the inner order of your life through the practice of temperance, because it is through that inner order, through self-control, that you are able to have the base to move outward to help other people. If your inner life is in chaos and disorder, you will not have the strength to help others. You will be more likely to be pulled down with them or pull them down with you. Most likely of all, you won't have the emotional bandwidth to care about them in the first place. Temperance gives you the serenity to love your neighbor.

So the discipline of temperance involves a turn inward to examine ourselves to see how we have ordered our desires and habits, questioning what end those desires and habits serve. Do they serve our selfless self-preservation (which glorifies God and is loving to our neighbor) or do they merely serve our selfish passions? Put differently, are our loves ordered according to the good as defined by God or are they ordered according to the world, the flesh, or the devil? We do this work of revelation with the aid of the Holy Spirit, our God-given faculties of reason, and the wise counsel of trusted friends. This requires time for contemplation and reflection about our habits, practices, thoughts, and attitudes. Once we have identified ways in which our inner lives and habits are disordered, our task is to prayerfully submit these disorders to God and ask for the fortitude to reorder our desires and habits toward God's will, to practice the virtue of temperance, which can only truly be practiced with the spiritual aid of the Holy Spirit working in our lives.

PRINCIPLES FOR TEMPERANCE IN THE MODERN WORLD

I want to introduce two postures toward our desires that I believe can aid us in developing the virtue of temperance. Both are opposed to our cultural norms, so they will take a great deal of intentionality to practice, but I have found them to be fruitful and rich guiding lights in my own life.

You must choose not to do all that you can do. Historically, the need for temperance was eased by lack of availability and opportunity. For example, before the internet, if you wanted to look at pornography, you could, but it took effort. Whereas today, it takes effort *not* to see pornography. There were certainly other temptations in the past, but I'm merely pointing out that there has been a seismic change, and that change is so great that we cannot just say that people have always been tempted to look at porn. We have never had this kind of access to our indulgences before. Whatever food you want, whatever images of naked bodies you want, whatever entertainment you want, is available and calling out to you. We are trained from a very young age to say "Yes!" to our desires, while our faith tells us that we must deny ourselves.

The French sociologist Jacques Ellul, in his essay "The Ethics of Non-power," tries to sort through a response to the critique of technique he lays out in *The Technological Society*: "[M]an will agree not to do all he is capable of."[17] *Technique* is the maximization of efficiency in every sphere of human activity. The idea is that in the modern world, efficiency has become our highest value. In some cases, it seems to be our only value. Values like love, justice, beauty, and humanity have fallen under the superior power of efficiency. *The Technological Society* paints a fairly grim picture of life in the modern world—a picture that is stifling, violent, controlling, and inevitably governed by *technique*.

But in "The Ethics of Non-power," Ellul argues that there is indeed a way forward, although it is not the triumphalist way we expect. Rather than a strategy for removing *technique* from the center of public life, Ellul argues that we individually and collectively need to make choices that deny ourselves positions of power. In other words, *we must choose not to do all that we can do*. The world will always invite us to do more, to have more, to experience more, to consume more. And it is our task to prudently decide which opportunities to deny ourselves.

Can you buy the latest phone? Yes. But you can also choose not to.

Can you eat out instead of making a home-cooked meal? Yes. But you can also choose not to.

Can you buy an expensive car that is harmful to the environment? Yes. But you can also choose not to.

Can you watch this pornographic film? Yes. But you can also choose not to.

Can you flirt with this person who is not your spouse? Yes. But you can also choose not to.

Can you join this new social media platform? Yes. But you can also choose not to.

Can you use AI to write this sermon? Yes. But you can also choose not to.

Exercising your choice to *not* participate is a form of radical resistance in a society that pressures us to always participate. Electing not to participate is difficult, but necessary. It reorients your desires by discipling your self-denial muscle. In 2 Peter 2:14 it describes false teachers who have "hearts trained in greed," but I think such training is the basic form of education for all Westerners today. Our advertising, markets, and entertainment cultivate envy and greed in our hearts, such that our self-denial muscle never develops unless we intentionally exercise it.

And it is a muscle we are called as Christians to exercise, daily. As Christ reminds us in Luke 9:23, "If anyone would come after me, let him deny himself and take up his cross daily and follow me." Self-denial is at the heart of Christian living, but I fear we have forgotten that in the decadent West. Self-denial begins with issues of grave importance, namely sin, but also includes issues of prudence, where there is not necessarily sin involved, but we are called to use wisdom to live our lives prudently for "the days are evil" (Ephesians 5:16).

So in the above examples, self-denial looks like not flirting with someone who is not your spouse (clear sin), but it also may look like not joining TikTok (a wisdom issue). Here's what's interesting: When you are not in the habit of practicing self-denial on the wisdom issues, you shouldn't be surprised that you struggle to deny yourself on the sin issues. Self-denial is a habit that must be practiced daily, which is why Christ called us to pick up our crosses daily. It's a lifetime of dying to self we are called to. Temperance involves the choice to practice self-denial, to choose not to do all that you can do, using prudence and the Holy Spirit as a guide.

Renunciation in affirmation not resignation.[18] At the heart of the challenge of temperance is the issue of desire. Desiring the wrong things or desiring good things in the wrong way. So how do you deal with the problem of inordinate desire? Hardly anyone talks about this problem, but the world is filled with beautiful, interesting, lovely people, and to be faithful to the law of Christ, you are to be married to one person (barring the obvious circumstances like death, adultery, abandonment, or abuse). Of all the wonderful people who exist in this world, you must learn to be content with one. That's remarkable. It is a spiritual discipline.

We either learn to be content with one person or with no one—at least not in the intimacy of marriage. Either way, contentment is key, the radical prospect of being content with what you have. That's the virtue of temperance in marriage. But even after marriage people don't stop being amazing and wonderful and fascinating. You will continue to meet people who draw your gaze with their physical beauty, their laugh, their wit and charm. What do you do about the fear of missing out as it is applied to love? I think the key is *renunciation in affirmation not resignation*. And this applies to more than just love.

We must learn to renounce things that feel right and good and safe for us, because they aren't good. Opportunities. People. Experiences. Products. All kinds of things in this life will be available to us and yet we'll be required to say "no," to renounce our desires, even when they are closer than our own skin. Life is the long process of renunciation or it is a kind of death of excess. Renunciation is often painful; it requires that you give up things you hold dear. That relationship that feels perfect. That job that pays so well. That honor that would fill you with pride, and that is precisely why you must give it up. Renunciation is another name for picking up your cross and dying daily for Christ. Renunciation is particularly difficult in a culture that trains you from the earliest age to say "Yes!" to all your desires.

But not all forms of renunciation are temperate. Some forms turn quickly into bitterness and malice. It is not enough to renounce a sports car because it is a waste of money. You bitterly loathe people who own them. It is not enough to renounce the beauty of another person, you maliciously mock them and imply vicious things about their promiscuity or intelligence. This is what I would call renunciation in *resignation*. You are resigned to your poverty or lack and you hate others for it. You are bitter toward the goodness that you cannot have—and most goodness in life you cannot have.

Renunciation in affirmation is the choice to say "It is good that you exist" to whatever you desire. "It is good that you exist and it is good that you are not mine." As we will learn when we discuss love in chapter seven, the definition of love is the affirmation of the existence of someone or something. Renunciation in affirmation is a choice, a posture that you choose, not something that happens to you. You must choose to affirm the goodness of something or someone who is not yours, despite your longing, despite your dreams and imagination. You affirm the goodness of the person or thing because it exists and because it is objectively good that it exists, even if subjectively it doesn't exist *for your sake*.

And why should it? Why should all the beauty in the world be there for you to partake in? In a very practical way, renunciation in affirmation not resignation is an application of Ellul's admonition for us to choose not to do all that we can do. I stress the role of agency in renunciation because we do have a choice to follow our desires very often. We live in a free and open society that invites and sometimes insists that we partake of the desires of our hearts, even or especially when it involves us getting into debt to do so. At those moments, it is the choice we make to deny ourselves, to renounce what feels good, that defines our virtue of temperance. It is the choice not to do all that we can do.

TEMPERANCE APPLIED

Smartphones and social media. One of the basic operating assumptions of modern people is that whatever new and exciting technologies are invented are free to be used and enjoyed by us unless they are explicitly and empirically proven to be harmful—and even then we prefer to see evidence of *physical* harm or at least measurable harm, certainly not moral or spiritual harm. When a new, popular device or technology is developed, we rush to adopt it, assuming that it is licit. But if we live in an environment which falsely assumes that we are our own and belong to ourselves, then we should expect that the products of this culture will be disordered accordingly. Our technology will inevitably be marked by this false anthropology. So our basic posture toward innovation should not be one of openness and excitement, but prudent skepticism and restrained interest.

The explosion of TikTok is a great example of this dynamic. By the time experts were warning about the dangers of TikTok, it was already a wildly successful platform with over a billion users. It was, to use the language of the 2008 financial crisis, "too big to fail." The social cost of opposing TikTok and of taking legal action to block its use in the United States has been too great for most politicians, even though we know that our data is being funneled by TikTok to a communist country that is openly antagonistic toward the United States and its citizens. And even though the psychological effects of the platform are well known: the way it feeds users radical views, the way it addicts users, the way it promotes unhealthy lifestyles, etc.[19]

To their credit, in April of 2024 the US Congress was able to pass a ban of the social media platform to take effect in January of 2025, but then President Trump delayed the ban through executive order, and there seemed to be no political will to challenge the president's order. Most politicians appear hopeful that

ByteDance, the Chinese company that currently owns TikTok, will agree to sell to an American company, but that will only leave us with the same addictive app and with the same harmful effects on young people, just without our data being sent to a communist country. I don't know what exactly will happen with TikTok in the coming years, but I do know that we cannot depend on our government to protect us from toxic technology—technology that is hostile to our humanity. We must choose to be temperate in our use, even while the producers of that technology are encouraging us to reflexively adopt it.

Skepticism and restrained interest does not require you to be a luddite and abandon your smartphone (although that is an option), but it does require a new posture toward technology adoption. Just because a new device or technology comes out doesn't mean you need to adopt it. Again, you must choose not to do all that you can do—intentional limitation. With each new device and service we must pause and ask ourselves, how will this thing alter my desires and habits? What end does it serve? Will it contribute to my selfless self-preservation or my self-denigration? Society will pressure us to ask *none of these questions*. Like a high-pressure salesman, society says, adopt, adopt, adopt! But temperance calls us to use prudence to weigh our uses of devices and services for God's glory, the common good, and our own good.

It is not just owning a smartphone that is the problem, however, but what we do with our smartphones and our computers, and the reality for too many of us is that we are addicted to our devices and the social media platforms on them. A kind of vicious feedback loop has been created where we feel lonely in the modern wasteland so we turn to social media for connection, which isolates us from the real world further, making us feel more lonely and more likely to turn to social media for solace. This is how addictions work.

I think there are many reasons why we turn to social media. Sometimes it is because we can't stand to be alone with our own thoughts and are afraid of being convicted of our sins, but a great many others are turning to social media as a coping mechanism to survive an inhuman environment. In the end, however, we still have the same basic problem: We are addicted. And even the person who recognizes that they are not their own but belong to Christ will continue to struggle with the pressures of this inhuman environment and the temptation to be addicted. This is where the virtue of temperance is so important. We need to exercise self-control over our use of technology.

Practically speaking, some of us will be more prone to addiction than others, which means that for some people a temperate use of social media may look like setting a hard time limit and certain boundaries around when it can be accessed (not before prayer and reading the Bible in the morning, not at the dining table, not when talking with someone, not before bed, etc.), whereas other people may need to cut out social media entirely. If you find that you cannot moderate your use of social media, then social media is not something you need in your life.

I don't have a set of perfect guidelines that will fit everyone's life for how they should use or not use social media and smartphones, but I do believe this: We are all called to practice the virtue of temperance. Practically, that means perpetual self-evaluation with the aid of the Holy Spirit, setting of clear boundaries, and acting on those boundaries. The process of self-evaluation needs to be an honest one. Are you out of control with your use of your smartphone? Can you resist checking your text messages? Can you walk somewhere or ride an elevator without reflexively needing to pull out your phone? Can you be on Instagram without scrolling for a half an hour? Do you make time for checking in on your mobile games or social accounts but not for prayer or the Word? In other words, can you exercise self-control over your device and these social media platforms, or do they control you?

If the answer is the latter, then what steps do you need to take to practice temperance and regain control of your life, even if it hurts for a time? Here is where the virtue of temperance calls on the prior virtue of fortitude for strength. We must be willing to suffer technology withdrawals and anxiety for the good of our overall mental, spiritual, and physical health, all of which are negatively affected by an addiction to social media or smartphones. The goal of temperance is to achieve an inner order, which we cannot do if our minds are colonized by technologies of distraction that keep us from the kind of restful contemplation and prayer that Jesus modeled for us in the Gospels. Just as Jesus knew his limits and stepped away from the buzz of life to rest and pray, we need to know our limits and practice temperance.

Chastity. Probably the area of life most affected by the ideology that says we must affirm all of our desires is in sexuality. Because it is so intimate and personal, so potentially beautiful and affirming, so powerful and seductive, and perhaps most of all, because it is so lucrative and addicting, sexuality holds an inordinate sway over most modern people's lives. Entire industries are built up just to lure us into the grip of lust, and many children are exposed to pornography through smartphones and social media. Chastity, the practice of temperance applied to sexual desire, is regularly frowned upon in the wider society as mere "purity culture," which shames people for having normal, healthy, natural desires. These critics find chastity particularly harmful since the Bible teaches that sexual activity outside of consensual sex between a man and wife in the covenant of marriage is unchaste, or sin. And so most contemporary sexual practices fall into the category of unchaste, everything from lustful thoughts and pornography to masturbation, sex outside of marriage, same-sex sexual acts, and a host of other imaginable and unimaginable activities.

Part of what these critics are picking up on is the difficulty of living a chaste life. It is a high calling, and one that can only be practiced with the aid of the Holy Spirit as well as the theological virtues (which we shall soon get to), faith, hope, and love, that carry us when we fail and inspire us when we grow weary or are tempted. But ultimately, the criticism of chastity in our culture comes from the ideology that we are our own and belong to ourselves, and therefore we have a moral obligation to ourselves to fulfill our sexual desires whenever and wherever possible.

Any form of external restraint on our sexual desires is therefore perceived to be oppressive. I think what Pieper and Aquinas and even Aristotle before him would want us to see is that giving in to your passion is *oppressive*, it's being controlled by your desires rather than by reason and what is good.[20] True freedom in life comes from the ability to choose to do a good act based on your powers of reason (gifted by God and guided by the Holy Spirit), rather than being liberated from all external guides. In that sense, chastity, while it may *feel* constraining at times, is actually the path to sexual freedom.

Regrettably, in some churches, the way biblical sexual ethics has been taught is that we're all called to be chaste before marriage, but once we're in marriage, we're free from having to practice chastity so long as we don't commit adultery. This has placed an unrealistic burden on young people to hurry up and get married so they can be free from the struggle of purity. It has given the impression that chastity is a virtue for the young. In reality, chastity never stops being an important virtue in our lives. It must be practiced daily regardless of our marital status or sexual desires.

The person who is married must practice chastity by waiting for a time when they and their spouse can be intimate, which may be longer than they desire. That's a stretch of time requiring patient, chaste, waiting. No pornography. No masturbation. No lusting after coworkers or people on the street. Waiting. And there will be times in married life where, due to life circumstances, that wait may be a considerably long time. This is particularly true when physical or mental health issues come into play. And yet the call to chastity remains.

Similarly, the person who is same-sex attracted must practice chastity, whether they marry someone of the opposite sex or stay single. For all of us, as I mentioned earlier in this chapter, beautiful, interesting people will continue to enter our lives, and they may enter our lives while we are vulnerable, desiring sexual companionship or feeling dissatisfied with our partner or our committed singleness, and the temptation will arise to fulfill our desire and find comfort. And the world will tell us, "Yes!" And we will have to pray, "It is good that you exist and it is good that you are not mine." We are called to a lifetime of chastity. This is a hard teaching. Temperance is no easy virtue, but it is one we are called to, particularly sexual temperance, over and over again in Scripture (Hebrews 13:4).

To develop the virtue of chastity we need to first rely on the work of the Holy Spirit in our lives to work on our hearts, to purify us, to forgive us, and to strengthen us. We need to allow the truth of God's grace to deeply sink into our bones so that we know when we fail, Christ's mercy is there for us. While at the same time, we need to have the fortitude to resist temptation and the prudence to know when to flee, when to walk away from a computer, when to close a tab, when to avert our eyes, when to find something productive to do with our time.

For those who find themselves already addicted to pornography, the first step is finding professional help to break that addiction, talking to your pastor, and then seeking out an addiction program. For others, you may need to put security measures on your devices to block the porn as best you can. Whether you are a man or a woman, don't allow shame or guilt to hold you back from seeking the help you need to break the habits of addiction to pornography. Trust your story to someone wise and responsible, pray for healing, have courage, take active steps to cut off contact with the pornography, and accept God's grace and forgiveness for you. He loves you.

Beyond the challenge of pornography, we must be circumspect about the intentions and desires we have in our relationships, in person and online. Are you pursuing someone, oversharing with them, forming a romantic bond outside of your marriage, scrolling through their photos, or fantasizing about them? Do you find yourself bitterly comparing your spouse to someone else? The disorder of a covetous or lustful heart can lead to a world of sorrow. Pray for forgiveness. Ask God to bring you peace. Pray for contentment and prudence with your actions.

While these are good and prudent steps, you also need to practice making the decision not to engage with lustful or covetous thoughts when they appear. Just label them as a thought and return to whatever you were doing. Don't dwell on them or agonize over them. Quickly label them and move on with your day. The more attention you give them, the more power they have over your inner thought life. When you do find yourself tempted, try to focus your attention back on reality in the here and now.

Pieper argues that one of the effects of unchastity is that it robs us of prudence, specifically our ability to see reality.[21] We become so selfishly focused on our desire that we lose sight of what's going on in the here and now. Lust takes us out of the real world with its consequences. Often we can disenchant lust and see sin for the vileness it is if we slow down and use prudence to see reality. Yes, this person is beautiful, but if I were to have an affair with them, what would be the consequences? How much damage would that cause to them and to me and my family and others around me? Yes, this pornography is free and available and looks alluring, but the reality is by participating in this I am choosing to dehumanize another person, treating them as a tool for my pleasure.

In the heat of passion, it's not always easy to listen to reason, but that is why it's important not to be governed by passion. At the end of the day, chastity involves a choice point. There is a moment in time when you either turn from your sin or you turn toward it. The virtue of chastity is built up by choosing again and again with the aid of the Holy Spirit, day in and day out, to turn away from your sin. It is a lifetime's effort for all of us, an effort of ordering our desires according to God's will.

For many of us, temperance will be the most challenging of all the virtues to practice because it is the one most vehemently opposed by society and our economy. But a life without the discipline of temperance is a life of disorder and chaos, a life where our passions pull us in whichever direction they choose and we are helpless before our base, instinctual desires. Temperance may feel constraining at times, but it is true freedom, for without godly limits to guide us, we are lost and anxious, wandering from one unfulfilling desire to another.

As with all virtues, temperance can only be achieved through the work of the Holy Spirit sanctifying us and our intentional discipline to make temperate choices, whether in the use of our smartphones, or in chastity, or whatever desire we may have. Temperance has an endless number of applications. The question we must ask ourselves in any given situation is, "Is this desire rightly ordered according to God's will?" When we discover a desire in ourselves that is not ordered in harmony with God's will, then we can say it is intemperate and we need to reorder that desire.

I think what you will discover as you intentionally develop the virtue of temperance is that temperance in one area of your life makes it a bit easier to be temperate in other areas of your life. Whereas when you are in the practice of saying "Yes!" to all your desires, it is difficult to choose to stop in one specific area. Of course, it will still be difficult to deny yourself, but that is what we are called to in this life, daily self-denial. And that's a beautiful and freeing thing, when you come to understand it well.

5

BELIEVING SOUNDLY

I HAVE WATCHED WITH SADNESS as many of my peers have deconstructed their faith to the point of abandoning it entirely. A certain amount of deconstruction, narrowly defined, is healthy and good. Indeed, the Protestant Reformation can be described as one dramatic act of deconstructing medieval Catholicism and its excesses. If by deconstruction we mean a process of carefully analyzing unexamined beliefs, picking apart belief systems to rightly determine what is true, good, beautiful, and (most of all) from God, and what is false, evil, ugly, and (most of all) human, then deconstruction is something everyone should practice at some point.

But in our contemporary moment, that is rarely what is meant by deconstruction. Instead, it comes in the form of a hypercritical spirit that assumes various secular modern, progressive perspectives and then judges the Christian faith against those perspectives. For example, if you believe that sexual expression is an entirely private, personal choice between consenting adults and a primary means of expressing your identity, then the church's command to limit sex to within marriage between one man and one woman seems regressive—the kind of thing one deconstructs to liberate oneself. In this kind of deconstruction, the person assumes the truth of a progressive ideology (or some other secular ideology) and deconstructs Christianity. They are selective in what they are willing to view critically.

We must acknowledge with tears that some of those who deconstruct do so out of places of real harm caused by the church. This must be recognized, lamented, and justly rectified when possible. But it's also the case that sometimes churches "harm" individuals by teaching that pursuing personal pleasure through sin is immoral. In other words, we must be able to hold two truths at the same time: Some people are leaving the faith because they have been harmed by abusive leaders, hypocrites, and communities, and some people are leaving because they want to fulfill sinful desires.

It's even possible for both to be true within the same person. Some would argue that we can *only* acknowledge the former, and that to acknowledge the latter is an effort to gaslight or to dismiss the former. But reality requires us to accept that both can be true. The truth is that people deconstruct for a variety of reasons: watching their church support wicked political candidates with Scripture, not receiving good answers for pressing questions about the Bible or theology, making friends with someone in the LGBTQ community and becoming convinced that the biblical teachings on sexual ethics are wrong, and so on.

But I suspect that more people abandon their faith today simply because it no longer feels relevant or necessary. Christianity demands a great deal of us. As T. S. Eliot put it, "Costing not less than everything."[1] The prospect of dying to yourself is frightening in its expansiveness. With such a great cost, what do we receive in return? Community? You can get community at work, through a club, or through social media. Morality? How often has the church been on the "wrong side" of morality? Spirituality? You can be spiritual without being religious and giving up your Sunday mornings, not to mention tithes and offerings.

Why endure all this self-denial when the world is calling you to self-affirmation?

All unhealthy forms of deconstruction amount to the same thing: a failure to believe, a lack of faith. God, as he is revealed to us through his Word, seems false, unbelievable, incongruous with the nature of the world as we know it. This unbelief comes easy to us not only because it is part of our sin nature to deny God, but also because our society functions under the assumption that God is absent. Our laws assume no divine authority. Our justice system assumes no divine justice. Our social norms assume radical autonomy instead of the reality of our belonging to God and to each other. To disbelieve is natural and conforming to the flow of society.

Additionally, it is normal and healthy to have doubts about faith, as we shall see. Every saint has struggled with their faith at one point or another, has wrestled with passages in the Bible, has questioned God's love or providence, or has wondered if some point of doctrine is correct. What makes these doubts difficult in our time is that we have the pressure to disbelieve weighing on us heavily. In the Middle Ages, Christians had the same fundamental doubts, but they didn't have the pressing fear or temptation to fall into atheism or some other religion. That just wasn't an imaginable option for them in the same way it is for us.

For us living in a secular age, the possibility of not being a Christian is all we have ever known. As philosopher Charles Taylor notes, for the modern person, all belief systems are contested,[2] which means that when we have what has always been a normal doubt or question, we have the added anxiety that maybe this doubt means we are falling away.

So how do we believe? How do we have faith in a secular age? And what does it look like to deconstruct or doubt or question our faith in a healthy way?

FAITH DEFINED

During Christ's final minutes on the cross, he cried out to God the Father: "'Eli, Eli, lema sabachthani?' that is, 'My God, my God, why have you forsaken me?'" (Matthew 27:46). In that moment of agony and abandonment, Jesus knew he was taking on the sins of the world. His question was rhetorical, for he knew the reason for his sacrifice, and he knew that he could not be ontologically separated from the Father—but the question captures the torment of his *experience*. Yet despite his agony and experience of abandonment, Christ endured the pain in faith.

His questioning of God comes from Psalm 22, which begins with the very same cry of abandonment yet quickly shifts to confidence in God's faithfulness, "Yet you are holy, enthroned on the praises of Israel" (Psalm 22:3). The rest of the psalm includes a similar pattern of lament about feeling abandoned in the midst of troubles and yet trusting in the Lord. In other words, when Christ cries out, he quotes a psalm that wrestles with God and questions his providence but ultimately retains a faith in the person of God. This allusion to Psalm 22 shows us that while Christ felt forsaken, he believed in the faithfulness of the Father to care for him in his suffering. This is the virtue of faith.

The book of Hebrews gives us the biblical definition of faith in chapter 11 verses 1-3: "Now faith is the assurance of things hoped for, the conviction of things not seen. For by it the people of old received their commendation. By faith we understand that the universe was created by the word of God, so that what is seen was not made out of things that are visible." Faith is both "assurance" and "conviction" about something which is not immediately evident. The example given is the act of creation by God, which we could not have witnessed, although we can see the results. We take it on faith that God created the cosmos by his Word. There is also an element of longing with faith. We have assurance of things we hope for, promises that God has made.

Naturally, Pieper's definition of faith (which is translated in his book as "belief") is similar: "the formal subject of belief is what is not apparent to the eye, what is not obvious of its own accord, what is not attainable either by direct perception or logical inference."[3] But Pieper elaborates on this definition and addresses a question you might have been wondering about the "assurance" and "conviction" mentioned in Hebrews chapter 11: on what basis do we have this confidence? Is faith just the assertion of confidence without reason? That sounds like folly more than a virtue.

I think Pieper can help us here: "[T]o believe means: to regard something as true and real on the testimony of someone else. Therefore, the reason for believing 'something' is that one believes 'someone.'"[4] The *core* of belief is always believing some*one*, in this case, God. We can be assured of our hope because we believe God's promises. Calvin in his *Institutes* defines faith similarly: "[Faith] is a firm and sure knowledge of the divine favor toward us, founded on the truth of a free promise in Christ, and revealed to our minds, and sealed on our hearts, by the Holy Spirit."[5] We can have conviction of things not seen because God has spoken about them. The beauty of the Christian faith is to be believed ultimately because someone infinitely good, loving, and trustworthy has communicated it to us in his Word.

The choice to wholly believe in a person assumes that there exists someone outside of you that is infinitely greater than you who has spoken clearly. This is why we can never truly believe another human being in the full sense of the term. Our belief is always qualified: I believe that you are telling the truth, but I know you could be lying or misrepresenting facts. Pieper points out that any time we try to put our faith in a human, "something essentially inhuman is taking place."[6] Faith can really only be practiced in its full form with one being, God. And if there is a God who has spoken to us clearly, then it is actually natural, right, and appropriate for us to put our faith in him, to believe in him and his Word.

This focus on faith in the person of God is a helpful corrective to a logic-focused account of Christianity that seeks to prove the rationality of the religion to make faith more "reasonable" and appealing to the world. Instead, we are called to believe in the one who created rationality and allow that faith guide us. We believe in God's Word, but we don't believe those words *because* they are clever, traditional, comforting, or persuasive words on their own (although they are), but because they are *his Words*. It is out of our faith in God that we follow his Word. Practically, this means that when we come across a teaching that does not fit the contemporary social norms, for example the Bible's teachings on same-sex romantic relationships, we accept the Word's teachings as authoritative and true because of the one who gave us those words.

How do we come to have faith in a person? What draws us to Christ? Pieper's answer might surprise you: "We believe, not because we see, perceive, deduce something true, but because we desire something good."[7] This is not to say that there is no room for discussions about the historicity of the resurrection or the reliability of Scripture, but the driving force of faith is *will*, according to Pieper.[8] We choose to put our faith in someone because we desire the good. Now here, Pieper and I part ways. As a Catholic thinker, Pieper emphasizes free will and volition. In keeping with the Reformed tradition, I believe the Scriptures teach that we *don't* desire the good without the work of God calling us to Christ (John 6:44). But despite our theological differences, the experiential reality of turning our wills toward God remains the same: We come to faith in Christ because the Holy Spirit *draws* us to desire the good and gives us faith.

Even though God is the one who calls us, Christ commands each of us to make the decision to turn our wills toward God (Mark 1:15). That is the act of faith. Desire brings along with it a sense of love. We believe in God because he first loved us so that we desire his goodness and we love him in return. Through reading his Word, being in his creation, marveling at the wonder of other human beings, exalting in the miracle of life, and feeling our need for a redeemer, we desire his goodness and love. And so we have faith in him.

That is not to imply that belief has nothing to do with facts about reality. Without facts about Christ's birth, death, and resurrection, in just what would we have "faith"? As Pieper puts it, "If *everything* is said to be belief, then belief has been eliminated."[9] Belief presupposes knowledge about God's revelation, and based on that knowledge and our faith in God's Word, we believe in eternal life, and the resurrection, and his laws, and his love for us. Belief also presupposes the work of the Holy Spirit exposing God's revelation to us, so that we see the truth of the gospel and are brought to repentance.

But that faith is not without doubts. As I mentioned earlier, doubts are normal, even Christ quoted a psalmist wrestling with God's providence when he was on the cross! Calvin writes that "we rather maintain that believers have a perpetual struggle with their own distrust, and are thus far from thinking that their consciences possess a placid quiet, uninterrupted by perturbation."[10] Doubts will come, whether they are doubts about how to interpret certain passages of the Bible, or how God could allow someone to suffer, or why God designed sexuality the way he did, or doubts about your salvation. And while it is virtuous to seek knowledgeable answers for these doubts, if we are fixed on the beauty and goodness and personhood of Jesus, through the work of the Holy Spirit we can have a "conviction of things not seen" (Hebrews 11:1). Because we have a conviction of the Person of Jesus, we can have doubts, uncertainty, without losing faith. The two are not mutually exclusive. We may not "see" the reason why a family member is allowed to suffer if God is good, but by turning our gaze upon Christ and his character we can have conviction that God *is* good. Doubts do not have to unsettle us. They may provoke us to investigate, but they do not have to unsettle our foundation, because our foundation is a Person, the Person of Christ. In that same passage in the *Institutes*, Calvin writes, "On the other hand, whatever be the mode in which they are assailed, we deny that they fall off and abandon that sure confidence which they have formed in the mercy of God."[11]

None of this is to suggest that such conviction is easy. It requires the work of the Holy Spirit in our lives making faith possible for us, pointing us to Christ, *giving* us faith. In these moments, we should turn to prayer. Our task is to practice that faith by choosing to look to Christ and to take steps of faith, living out our lives in accordance with his Word.

Note that this understanding of faith is not a blind leap in the dark. When I talk about accepting that doubts will occur and having faith anyway, and when the author of Hebrews talks about "convictions of things not seen" we are both grounding our faith *in a real, historic person*. Jesus. Believe even though you can't see everything, even though you can't have perfect certainty, even though you still have lingering doubts—believe because you have met a Person who is worthy of your complete trust.

In my own life, there have been many passages from the Bible that have caused me to wonder and doubt without shaking my faith. I accept uncertainty about how to interpret those passages or how God's goodness can be consistent with a particular action,

I pray to God for clarity and peace, and I move on. When I have time and the opportunity, I seek clarity from those spiritually wiser than myself about these doubts, but sometimes I'm still left with a mystery. And that is okay.

Our tendency is to obsess about how many doubts we have, but John Calvin reverses the focuses in his *Institutes* and encourages us to focus on how valuable just a little bit of faith can be: "As soon as the minutest particle of faith is instilled into our minds, we begin to behold the face of God placid, serene, and propitious; far off, indeed, but still so distinctly as to assure us that there is no delusion in it."[12] You may have only a particle of faith amid a cloud of doubts, but don't discount that particle. It is enough to begin to behold the face of God.

THE SOURCE OF FAITH

The virtue of faith allows us to know God and live more fully as human beings created by him. It is through faith that we are saved, and through faith that we are able to hope (as we shall see in the next chapter). Faith is part of the design of humanity. We were made to believe. It is not simply that we have faith that God exists in the abstract, but we engage with God through hearing his Word, and it is precisely that act of engaging with God's Word that develops faith. We read in Romans 10:17 that "faith comes from hearing, and hearing through the word of Christ." The aim of our faith is the person of God, and we grow in the virtue of faith by hearing the Word of God as communicated to us from God in Christ.

Remember that in faith we desire the goodness of God in love. Through reading and meditating on the Scriptures, we can see the beauty and goodness of God displayed. We can see his goodness in the act of creation at the beginning. I would even venture to suggest that creation itself, insofar as it is *Christ's* creation, is his Word also, or at least his revelation. Therefore we, like David sitting in the wilderness watching his flocks, can learn about God's goodness by meditating on creation. We can see God's goodness in sending his Son to earth to be incarnated as a man to live and die and rise again for the forgiveness of our sins. We can see his beauty in his laws, which enable us to live fully as we were created.

There is an endless wealth of goodness to be revealed in Scriptures about God the Father, God the Son, and God the Holy Spirit. By immersing ourselves in Scriptures and meditating on them, our faith is grown, not just in the sense of factual knowledge about the Bible, which is of great value in itself, but in *trust* in the *person* of God, which is the essence of faith.

FAITH APPLIED

Healthy deconstruction. I said earlier in this chapter that a healthy deconstruction should be practiced by everyone at some point, but I don't think it should be a continual process, which might shock some of you. I think it is a modern scientific perspective that says we should be in a continual process of revision. While it's important and valuable to examine your beliefs, there should be an "end of all our exploring," to quote T. S. Eliot again.[13] It's appropriate and even mature to come to a place where you have analyzed and critiqued enough. A place where you don't have all the answers and you haven't explored all the questions, but you've done enough to have the faith to move on, accepting something as true even though you aren't completely certain.

That doesn't mean you should be closed off to new information. Even the apostle Paul said that if Christ didn't rise from the dead, the entire faith is in vain (1 Corinthians 15:14). There are things that can disconfirm the Christian faith. But if by "faith" you mean that you must have every question about the Bible answered, you will be very tired and never satisfied. Such a collection of sixty-six books is bound to produce an endless number of questions, challenges, and seeming inconsistencies. I invite you to explore those challenges, but at a certain point, stop. Cease from your exploration. Accept your conclusions and act in faith.

By "ceasing" I don't mean stop asking questions, I mean stop putting off faith. It's good and proper to keep exploring if you do so *within* the posture of faith. Your questions change when you ask them from a posture of faith. They come not from a position of skepticism, but from a desire to see how a puzzle piece fits in a grand puzzle. And you don't always get to fit the piece, but in faith you see how the design is masterful, and you trust the designer. But the person who chooses to wait until all questions are answered before they commit to faith will never commit. They cannot even admit that there is a puzzle.

This is not merely a rule for religious belief. It is a rule for life. You can't wait for certainty before you act and commit. At some point, you must say, "I know enough," so I will marry this person. Or I know enough, so I will take this job. Or I know enough, I will order this meal, or cross this street, or buy this house. You must act without knowing for certain that your actions are perfectly wise, prudent, just, good, or beautiful. Knowing when to stop analyzing is a matter of prudence, but in the end, it's always going to be true that you won't know with absolute certainty.

This is especially true of matters of religious faith. You'll have to act in faith—even for something as big and life-defining as religious belief. Such an act of faith is the cornerstone to a healthy, meaningful, God-honoring life. The alternative is a kind of slow death, either because you deny the complexity of the situation and insist that you have a certain conclusion which you can't possibly have, or because you keep actively searching for an unachievable conclusion at the expense of actually living your life.

So please, ask good questions, and seek answers, but don't let your questions hinder you from faith. Take your questions with you. And if you don't get good answers from you pastor, don't take that to mean that no good answer exists. No one person can be an expert at everything. Everyone is just doing their best. If you don't get sufficient answers, seek out answers from someone who is more qualified. But at the end of the day, you'll eventually have to accept that there is an end to knowledge. That life is not lived finding all the answers. That faith does not come from plugging every hole your imagination can dream up about the Christian tradition. As I said before, nothing in life works that way, why should faith?

There are those who devote their lives to the critiquing of institutions, people, and beliefs, and there is no peace there. It is a sin of restlessness. Eventually, you must have faith in something or someone and act on that faith, whether it is faith that gravity will continue to operate according to certain physical laws or faith that there is a loving God who cares for you enough to send his Son to die for your sins. We can marshal all the evidence we want, but in the end we must act or be delusional or dead.

A perverse preoccupation with critiquing might be defined as *curiositas*, a lust for knowledge which can never be appeased—a lust for knowledge for the sake of gaining more knowledge, for the emotional thrill of accumulating it. Or this can look like criticism for the sake of criticism, a consumptive cynicism. The modern world sees *curiositas* as a virtue, but it's really a vice, an inordinate desire to master the world through the accumulation of knowledge. And there is no peace there.

Understood this way, faith is the basis of a healthy life. There is an element of temperance at work in a healthy faith. You must know how much analysis is appropriate and at what point your analysis of a situation, belief, or problem turns into an inordinate obsession, a failure to act. In that way there is also fortitude. To act in faith requires the courage to act, the courage to step out into the unknown. But such courage is grounded in faith in God's ultimate love for us, his preserving acts of compassion.

There should be an end to all your exploring, but there must also be a beginning, a time and place when you start the journey to explore your beliefs and their basis in Scripture and the traditions of the church. Some may object to my inclusion of traditions, but Scripture is always interpreted in context of a community, and the church is Christ's community here on earth across time and space. That is not to say that the community has always been right. As a child of the Protestant Reformation, I am well aware that the church often makes mistakes—sometimes grave mistakes. But I believe that the Holy Spirit is working through Christ's body to purify his bride, bringing her as a pure, righteous bride to the wedding feast of the Lamb. Our job is to be faithful.

As I mentioned in the introduction to this chapter, we live in what Charles Taylor describes as a highly contested age. This means we are likely to be tempted to change beliefs simply because the options are available to us. There is a temptation to view any conclusion, any end to our exploring, as arrogant. How arrogant of us to come to the conclusion that Christ is Lord of all! How could any of us ever come to such a conclusion when there are millions of belief systems available to us?

The modern person can be into Roman Catholicism one year, MMA the next year, competitive fishing the next year, Islam the next, Taylor Swift, Pokémon, video games, ultramarathons, racial injustice, couponing, and so on. There is no end to the lifestyle options available to us, which means that we are going to be inclined to constantly upgrade our faith as we upgrade our cellphones, trading up for the newer model when our old one feels inadequate or too demanding. Here we are back to the vice of *curiositas*, a rootless wandering in search of knowledge that will never satisfy.

Which is one reason why it's so important to carefully analyze the nature of our doubts. Not all doubts about faith come from authentic, meaningful, and reasonable sources. Sometimes people doubt the Christian faith because of a genuine skepticism about the reliability of Scriptures. Those doubts deserve attention from pastors, elders, biblical scholars, and theologians. Other times people *say* they doubt the faith because of a skepticism about the reliability of Scriptures, but really they find the demands of the faith too taxing, or they find the social cost of being associated with other evangelicals too much to bear. It's not your place to judge the sincerity of someone else's doubt. But it definitely *is* your place and responsibility to judge the sincerity of *your own* doubts. Doubt your doubts. Do not trust your heart, for it is wicked and deceptive.

A good practice is to pray for clarity. God is a good God who cares for his children. He will give you clarity about the nature of your doubt. When there are reasonable questions, pursue answers. When you discover bitterness, resentment, hurt, or fear in your heart, you may need to work through your emotions with a Christian therapist or pastor or both, rather than doubt your faith. The world will pressure you to adopt one practice after another, to progress from belief to belief in a quest for peace that will never come. Your duty is to be as honest with yourself as you can be about your doubts, to seek help with those doubts when you need help, but to hold fast to what you know to be true, because you know the one who communicated that truth, and he loves you.

Bitterness.[14] In addition to doubts, one of the challenges to walking in faith that is common to humanity is bitterness or anger toward God. We dislike admitting this to others and even to ourselves because it feels like blasphemy, yet the Bible is filled with examples of faithful, godly men and women who cried out in frustration to God. Christ himself asked that the cup of suffering and death be passed from him (Matthew 26:39)!

At one point or another in life you will be faced with a tragedy or circumstance that tests your faith in God's provision, his goodness, or his promises. Unfortunately, this may come through the work of those in the church, which can be particularly traumatic to process. How could God's body here on earth be used to harm and abuse me? History is littered with such stories, from the early church period to today, and it is only natural to turn that question to God himself: How could *you* allow *your* church to harm me?

I don't have answers to such questions, except to say that God will bring judgment on those who abuse his children and that God somehow works all things together for the good of those who love him (Romans 8:28). As unimaginable as that may seem, God is still working our good through our suffering. He is still caring for us. He loves us and sorrows over our harm (consider Jesus' tears over Lazarus in John 11:35). And he will see justice done, in this life or the next. There is no escaping his justice.

But those answers require faith, faith that God's promises are true. That he really *is* a God of justice and that he really *will* work all things together for our good. And this is where the tension lies. When you go through a period of suffering, whether from the church or not, it is faith itself that can become questionable. You begin to doubt God's justice. Doubt God's ability to work all things together for our good. How could any good come from this suffering, or if it can, why did God have to allow this suffering for this "good" to occur? What kind of God *is he*?

The refrain becomes the question, "Why God, why?" And this is where the virtue of faith and the work of the Holy Spirit as comforter must aid us. If we have our faith in a particular doctrine of God but not in his person, I'm afraid that in times like these we may feel the doctrines fail to answer our questions and then our faith will fail as well. But if we have immersed ourselves in Scripture and come to know, love, desire, and have faith in Christ and his Word, then as difficult as it may be to understand *why* this suffering is here, we can accept on faith that God is good. We can accept on faith that God is bringing his justice. We can accept on faith that God is working his good for us.

It's good for us to remember that accepting on faith requires the virtue of fortitude and may mean the sweating like drops of blood. As I mentioned earlier, at the Garden of Gethsemane Christ prayed that the cup of suffering and death might be passed from him but accepted that the Lord's will would be done (Luke 22:42). He prayed in anguish, desiring to obey God and yet not desiring to suffer death on the cross. Like Christ, we will be faced with many situations where we may turn to God in anguish and beg that the cup of suffering be taken from our lips, and we may have to drink anyway. He had faith in God the Father's will and goodness even while he desired not to have to suffer. Similarly, the path of faithfulness for us through times of trial requires us to believe in God's character and press on in fortitude, knowing the good and pursuing it.

This does not mean that the emotions of frustration or bitterness will vanish. You may continue to feel abandoned by God or neglected, and there is no shame or sin in expressing those emotions to God in the form of prayer or the reading of a psalm. David found great comfort in voicing his own anxieties about God, even while he continued to have faith (remember Psalm 22). And this is the duality we must learn to live with. Challenging God in prayer and begging him for rescue, or crying out for his justice, or asking him why he has allowed an injustice, or expressing your frustration does not mean that you have to lose faith in God.

We know this on the human level, but sometimes can forget it when it comes to God. When your good friend disappoints you in some way, you don't cease loving that friend, instead you express your hurt and seek reconciliation (if it's a healthy friendship). In other words, your trust in your friend is deeper than your hurt. So too is our frustration with God. Except your friend can truly betray you. God cannot. He loves you infinitely and gave his Son for you. He is preserving your existence this very moment, even if it is a moment of hurt and suffering.

Sometimes in bitterness and frustration we may cry out to God, "Lord, I do not understand why I must endure this. I do not see your goodness at work in this situation, but I choose to have faith in your goodness." In such moments we come to see that faith is not an emotion, but an act of the will, a decision we make to commit ourselves to trust another person. Our emotions may run wild and object to this trust and demand immediate answers and justice and peace, but we can use our wills to choose faithfulness anyway. It may be that we need to pray the prayer, "Lord, I believe, help my unbelief," but that is not a contradiction (Mark 9:24). Faith in God includes aspects of unbelief because we are weak, fallen creatures who are growing in our faith. So as with any virtue, we desire more of that virtue, more faith. Perhaps you believe rationally or with conviction but disbelieve emotionally or viscerally. Your prayer is that God will take that part of you that still believes and breathe life into it.

It is by faith that each of us is saved (Ephesians 2:8), learning to put our trust in the one who created all things and died for our sins and who has spoken to us through his Word. That faith will be tested through natural doubts and cynical doubts, through suffering and trials. The one who perseveres will be committed to hearing the Word and meditating on it to know the person of God. They will develop this virtue over time through the continual decision to turn their will toward God in trust and obedience and through the work of the Holy Spirit. And they will have the faith to wrestle with God and come out still loving and trusting him.

6

HOPING RESOLUTELY

IN JACQUES ELLUL'S *Hope in Time of Abandonment*, he notes that contemporary people (in the 1970s, when the book was written) hold two contrary visions of the world. On the one hand they see the world as hopelessly unchanging and out of their control. They are helpless to affect the structures of the world, whether it be technology or the government or mass entertainment. Everything is too large and too powerful to change. I'm not sure what he had in mind in 1970, but today I think about the monstrous forces of smartphones and social media, which seem to be these unstoppable juggernauts, crushing anyone who abstains from them. Here we are with smartphones and the internet and nothing is going to change that.

On the other hand, Ellul says contemporary people are confronted with "everything, it would seem, . . . changing at high speed,"[1] such that it's impossible to avoid a kind of vertigo. Ellul has in mind here the changes brought to us by the news, and certainly those have only accelerated since the '70s with the advent of the internet, but what has also accelerated are social norms. What is acceptable to say in public and what views are considered offensive have rapidly changed over the last decade in America.

Ellul concludes: "This twofold experience happens at one and the same time to the same person. He experiences the two parts together and cannot deal with them. Both bring him to the same resignation through the absence of a prospect for the future."[2] That last sentence is the key to understanding why it is so difficult to practice the virtue of hope in the contemporary world: It is difficult for us to imagine a hopeful future. We can imagine things roughly continuing the way they always have: The wars in the Middle East will continue, technology will continue to invade more and more spaces in our lives, the government will continue to be inept, and so on. And we can imagine things radically out of our control: Shocking new technology like AI, natural disasters possibly caused by climate change, unprecedented presidents, and so on. But we struggle to imagine a hopeful future, a future where our deepest human hopes are meaningfully fulfilled.

That is not to say that people today have no form of hope. Hope, as we shall discover, involves a positive orientation toward the future, and many people today fit that very rough description. For example, activists fighting against injustice are acting in hope that one day the world will be a more just place. Billionaires who invest their wealth in space travel are acting in hope that one day we might colonize Mars and save the human race from extinction.[3] Effective altruists act in hope that by manipulating people and efficiently spending massive amounts of wealth, we can preserve humanity or the environment or both. Techno-optimists believe that with advances in AI, we can solve humanity's problems. All of these are hopes for the future. But I think we can narrow many of the modern forms of hope down to two: hope in efficiency and hope in secular justice.

Hope in efficiency is the belief that with enough time, energy, and resources, we can use techniques to master our universe and create some kind of utopia. Perhaps that utopia is a society where AI-controlled robots do all the labor and humans are free to endlessly explore reality (virtual or otherwise). One where humans live significantly longer and age significantly slower (which naturally means assisted suicide becomes the standard cause of death). The point is there is a *vision* to this technological hope which efficiency will bring us to. All we have to do is set aside our morality, red tape, and regulations so that the innovators can get to work creating the future.

This (false) hope is one of the challenges to cultivating the true virtue of hope in the contemporary world, because we are easily seduced by it. So much of our society is built around the advancement of technology and the promotion of efficiency that it is easy for us to put our hope in them to save us. But while technology has brought about great good in our world, and we can hope for it to bring more good, it cannot bear the weight of hope that we need it to. Efficiency is too small of a thing to save us. Technology is too fragile to hope in.

One significant reason we cannot put our hope in technology is that it is indifferent to humans and morality. The march of innovation and efficiency does not ask whether we ought to create brain implants that connect us to the internet all the time, or smartphones that do the same thing, or platforms like TikTok that are addictive by design. Innovation and efficiency only ask if it's possible and profitable. Morality is subsumed under "progress." To have a human hope, we need a hope that respects our humanity. And technology will not do.

Justice, however, is all about humanity. And many people hope in a human form of justice that I would call secular social justice. All justice is by nature *social*; it's about our relationships between each other and God. But there is a type of *secular* social justice that owes more to certain Marxist ideological commitments than to Christian theories of justice. A problem with this particular form of hope is that it often has no ultimate *telos*, no final hopeful arrival, only the endless, daily grind of upsetting the new power structures. There will always be some oppressed group because there will always be some sort of power dynamic in the world, so justice becomes a process of hunting for the next group in power to oppose. There is no hope for redemption or restitution or repentance or peace, not even in Christ. Only perpetual conflict between groups. As you can imagine, this kind of hope is not really hope at all, but despair, and it leads to cynicism, suspicion, frustration, and burnout.

However, the call to justice, as we have seen in chapter two, is real. We *are* called by God to advocate for the oppressed. Even though perfect justice cannot be achieved in this life by *us*, Christ *can* and *will* bring it about in his time, and we are still responsible for working toward justice despite our inability to reach perfection. In fact, we should be striving for prodigal justice to make the world more human. But the striving for prodigal justice I'm describing is not the same as the endless fighting against power structures that marks secular social justice causes. The difference is the end of our prodigal justice is Christ's triumphal return, and the "end" of upsetting power structures is always going to be the discovery of more power structures to upset. One ends in the wedding feast of the Lamb, the other in frustration.

But there is tremendous social power behind secular social justice causes. They have weight and social significance behind them. To be opposed to a secular social justice cause feels like being on the "wrong side of history," which feels alienating and shameful. It's tempting to adopt these causes as your form of hope, but as with techno-optimism, secular social justice cannot hold the weight of our need for true hope. It falls short in this case because it has no true vision of completion. There is no *telos* toward which it is moving.

Another difficulty in having hope in the modern world is that everything seems to be aimlessly wandering into some unknown and ungovernable future, which returns us to Ellul's point about living with the tension between nothing changing and uncertainty. I'm reminded of Peter's warning in 2 Peter 3:4, "They will say, 'Where is the promise of his coming? For ever since the fathers fell asleep, all things are continuing as they were from the beginning of creation.'" That is what it feels like, everything is continuing without resolution, without justice, without peace, without the second coming. Life just goes on, and here you are, stuck in the middle of it. The mundane nature of life can make it difficult to hope. It doesn't help that our lives are so busy and hectic that we hardly have time to reflect on what we are doing or why. I suspect that many of us aren't driven by the virtue of hope but by deadlines and schedules and obligations. Hope seems too far off, too hypothetical, true hope at least.

HOPE DEFINED

In the Gospel of John, right before Jesus' betrayal by Judas, Jesus prays the High Priestly Prayer over his disciples and the coming believers who will make up the church. In this prayer we can see Jesus' hope in God's promises manifested:

> Holy Father, keep them in your name, which you have given me, that they may be one, even as we are one. While I was with them, I kept them in your name, which you have given me. I have guarded them, and not one of them has been lost except the son of destruction, that the Scripture might be fulfilled. But now I am coming to you, and these things I speak in the world, that they may have my joy fulfilled in themselves. I have given them your word, and the world has hated them because they are not of the world, just as I am not of the world. I do not ask that you take them out of the world, but that you keep them from the evil one. They are

> not of the world, just as I am not of the world. Sanctify them in the truth; your word is truth. (John 17:11-17)

Christ knew he was about to leave his disciples behind to face an overwhelming task—to spread the gospel across the face of the earth among hostile people who would persecute and martyr them. In hope, he prays to God the Father that they would be kept near to God, that they would be united, that they would be kept from the evil one, and that they would be sanctified in the truth. Jesus was confident that God would fulfill these requests because of God's goodness. This is the virtue of hope.

Hope is many things. Hope is a vision for tomorrow that doesn't allow the chaos of today to overshadow it. Hope asserts the goodness of the future, even when the future feels unimaginable. Hope is a leap in the dark, the deep belief that today's troubles will not define the future, however much they may trouble us today. Hope is rising out of bed in the morning and taking that step to the block. Hope is defiance of sin, evil, and sorrow. Hope asserts that "it is good!" Hope is not the same thing as a positive outlook or optimism. Hope can be steely faced and realistic about a potential negative outcome of any particular event, but it denies the finality of that event. Even in the death of a loved one, there is hope for the resurrection.

Hope believes that God is making all things new through the power of his resurrection. God is making all things new, redeeming all things, healing, which doesn't mean that no harm will occur or no suffering from our mistakes. It means that suffering will be made perfect through Christ's work. Somehow. "Somehow" is the language of hope. "Somehow" defies the finality of the world. Hope drags you through discouragement and despair. Hope is the embodiment of possibility. Hope refuses to allow despair to have the last word. Hope is an obligation that demands much of you, it requires the fortitude to endure when others invite you to surrender.

But hope is also a form of surrendering, surrendering to the power of God to redeem this life, your life. Hope does not deny the reality of suffering, but only its final power. Hope is not dependent on information. It does not require certainty but calls us on to perseverance in the face of adversity and the unknown. Hope is a virtue because it must be cultivated and enacted. It requires practice and conscious decisions. Some people are temperamentally optimistic, but optimism is not the same thing as hope. Hope lives on even when optimism dies. The basis of optimism is a positive assumption about the outcomes of situations, which is not grounded in the nature of reality. The basis of hope is the life, death, and resurrection of Christ Jesus, which is the ground of reality.

Hope is like faith in that it involves a confidence in something unseen, but whereas faith involves a confidence in some*one* unseen, hope is in an unseen future fulfillment. It is a specific orientation toward the future: "Hope, like love, is one of the very simple, primordial dispositions of the living person. In hope, man reaches 'with restless heart,' with confidence and patient expectation, toward . . . the arduous 'not yet' of fulfillment, whether natural or supernatural."[4] Pieper makes the distinction between natural and supernatural hope, but I would add that the ultimate form of hope is hope in Christ's second coming and the resurrection of the dead.

All other forms of hope, supernatural and natural, are merely shadows of that one essential hope. A natural hope would be the hope to get a raise in your job, whereas a supernatural hope might be to see a loved one healed of a sickness. There is nothing wrong with natural hopes. We all have them, but Pieper notes that ultimately, "hope, as a virtue, is something wholly supernatural."[5] I take him to mean here that even natural hope has its final basis in the supernatural hope in a loving God.

A key to hope is this concept of "not yet," the patient waiting for fulfillment of some rightly desired thing. There is something about this waiting that is actually ennobling: "[H]ope, as the lasting elevation of man's being, cannot exist except from, through and in Christ."[6] Divine hope is not only the "not yet" waiting for fulfillment, it is the *current* fulfillment of what we were created for! We were created to hope in Christ, for "Christ is the actual foundation of hope."[7] In hope we enact our faith in the One who is worthy of hope and we practice fortitude, enduring the "not yet" with courage and driven by love.

We can see an example of hope modeled in Paul's writing in Romans chapter 8 verses 22-25:

> For we know that the whole creation has been groaning together in the pains of childbirth until now. And not only the creation, but we ourselves, who have the firstfruits of the Spirit, groan inwardly as we wait eagerly for adoption as sons, the redemption of our bodies. For in this hope we were saved. Now hope that is seen is not hope. For who hopes for what he sees? But if we hope for what we do not see, we wait for it with patience.

For Paul, our hope is in the redemption of our bodies through Christ's work on the cross, a hope even creation longs for. Note that there is an element of uncertainty in this hope. Hope is veiled in an unknown future. We don't know when fulfillment will occur, so we must "wait for it with patience."

That is what hope looks like. Waiting with patience. Even though we don't know *when* this redemption will occur, we can be comforted that it *will* occur. Paul in Philippians 1:6 writes, "And I am sure of this, that he who began a good work in you will bring it to completion at the day of Jesus Christ." Paul said these words in *hope*. He was "sure" that God would complete his good work in them, saving them to the day of Christ's coming, and that surety rested on hope in God through the "not yet."

Hope is not primarily a feeling, although it sometimes may be that. But the virtue of hope is an action, a practice that we cultivate over time and through the work of the Holy Spirit by making the decision to live in relation to the future with the confident belief that Christ is returning with justice, Christ is making all things new, and Christ will resurrect our bodies from the dead. We make decisions and take actions based on that hope, not despairing regardless of what the world or our feelings predict.

One practical way we practice hope is through prayer: "Prayer and hope are naturally ordered to each other. Prayer is the expression and proclamation of hope."[8] As we pray for our needs and the needs of others, we allow God to show his ability to meet our needs according to his perfect will and we learn to wait in hope for the fulfillment of our desires.

Hope is deeply related to the virtue of fortitude, because hope is what gives fortitude the strength to carry on. Hope says that tomorrow is worth fighting for, despite all contrary evidence. And there will be contrary evidence. As we discussed in chapter three, life inevitably involves a great deal of suffering, and hope says there is meaning in that suffering, even if that meaning cannot be understood this side of paradise.

The apostle Paul gives us some idea of the meaning of suffering, however, and its relationship to hope in 2 Corinthians 4:16-18:

> So we do not lose heart. Though our outer self is wasting away, our inner self is being renewed day by day. For this light momentary affliction is preparing for us an eternal weight of glory beyond all comparison, as we look not to

> the things that are seen but to the things that are unseen. For the things that are seen are transient, but the things that are unseen are eternal.

Suffering, this "momentary affliction," prepares us for "an eternal weight of glory beyond all comparison." But that weight of glory is in "things that are unseen," things we must hope in because they are yet unfulfilled. Of course this does not mean that suffering is trivial, but it does have meaning. And through a fortitude grounded in hope we can endure that suffering.

Despair and presumption are the twin vices of hope.[9] In despair we give up all hope and in presumption we assume that we don't need hope because we have already attained fulfillment. Either way, these vices close off the "not yet" nature of hope and leave us with a false sense of certainty.[10] In some ways, we can see these dangers at work in the two challenges I discussed above: efficiency and secular social justice. In the case of the techno-optimist, there is a kind of presumption at work, a belief that we don't need to rely on hope in a divine savior to bring peace, justice, and salvation to humanity. We can create a utopia ourselves, given enough time and wealth. And as we have already seen with the secular social justice movement, there is a kind of despair at work that assumes there can never be peace, never be shalom, never be justice, only more striving.

In our own lives we may fall into despair or presumption, believing that God cannot or will not save us or that we have won our salvation through our good works. Here is a place I depart strongly from Pieper, whose deep Catholicism leads him to condemn the Reformed doctrines of grace as a sin of heresy and presumption. Pieper cannot seem to conceive of the possibility that Christians can continue to hope *and* have assurance of salvation. But there is no contradiction here. While our justification is fulfilled, our resurrection, glorification, and Christ's second coming are "not yet." Existentially (which is what troubles Pieper), we experience our faith as pilgrims, on the way, "not yet" arrived, but in some sense assured of our arrival by God's grace. And all this assurance happens through and in hope in Christ.

While presumption is a dangerous vice that anyone can fall into, it seems to me the less common vice in our time. The contemporary person is less likely to think that they have arrived or fulfilled themselves than that they are constantly insufficient, inadequate, and insecure. Certain movements, like the hypermasculine hustle culture that you can find on Instagram and YouTube—which includes weight lifting, expensive cars, investing, and extreme discipline—exemplify this presumption, as they seem to assume that we can achieve a mastery over our minds and bodies to reach our best lives now.

Then there are wealthy figures like billionaire Bryan Johnson who have devoted themselves to extending their lives indefinitely through a rigorous routine of exercise, diet, and medical procedures.[11] That too is a kind of presumption, a belief that through science and willpower, in the case of Johnson, he has already achieved fulfillment (so long as he keeps up the routine!). Contemporary efforts to optimize the body, to achieve upper-middle-class status (or higher), or to live an Instagrammable lifestyle are all examples of presuming that your hope is already fulfilled in the here and now. But it strikes me that these are the exceptions that prove the rule that presumption is less common than despair. Few of us can afford the vice of presumption, but despair is available to everyone.

The vice of despair can take many forms in our lives, but whatever shape it takes, it is destructive and soul-destroying. Pieper notes that despair refers to "a decision of the will. Not a mood, but an act of the intellect. Hence not something into which one falls, but something one posits."[12] This is a helpful distinction to make for those of us who are prone to melancholy emotions. Our *moods* are not the concern here. You can be happy and in despair! In fact, many people who are happy are in profound despair according to Pieper's usage of the term. The person who happily gambles his life away is in despair, for instance.

What matters is the decision of our wills, our intellect. What are we choosing to believe and act on? "Both he who hopes and he who despairs choose these attitudes with their will and let them determine their conduct."[13] This view of hope gives tremendous agency to the individual, and I would add to it that supernatural hope, the hope in the fulfillment of God's promises, requires the work of the Holy Spirit. But we still have to make a choice to hope.

Even as Christians with the power of the Holy Spirit, we can abandon hope and choose despair. And when we do so, it manifests in our *conduct*. We cease making meaningful plans for the future. We stop taking care of ourselves. We give up looking for a spouse or job. We give in to sinful impulses because we assume that we can't be saved anyway. We waste our resources because we no longer care about tomorrow. It can show up in a million different actions. But the key is, despair is a decision of the will to not hope in the fulfillment of God's promises (foremost his promises of redemption) and actions which reflect that loss of hope.[14]

What makes despair so unbearable is that we never cease to desire fulfillment, we just suppress it: "In despair man actually denies his own desire, which is as indestructible as himself."[15] Despair, then, puts us in conflict with ourselves. We desire fulfillment, yet we deny ourselves that desired fulfillment by giving up hope in it. For example, we desire justice, but after seeing so many acts of injustice in the world, we fall into despair and give up on justice ever being accomplished. We desire redemption and justification, but after sinning and sinning we convince ourselves that God could never redeem us, so we deny ourselves hope in Christ's fulfilled work on the cross. Despair is a seductive and destructive force in the lives of many people today.

One way we resist the temptation to turn to presumption or despair is by practicing hope in community. In communities of hope we encourage each other to patiently wait in the "not yet" for fulfillment of God's promises. We meet weekly to remind each other that we are waiting together with eager and confident expectation for the second coming of Christ. In my Presbyterian tradition, as a part of the liturgy before the Lord's Supper, we collectively recite, "Christ has died, Christ has risen, Christ will come again," reminding us of who our hope is in and what fulfillment we are hoping in. Even more fundamentally, in the ancient creeds like the Nicene and Apostles' Creeds, we speak words of hope together with believers across time and space, language and culture. In this way, the Christian virtue of hope is never ultimately a private act, but a corporate act, which we embody personally.

HOPE APPLIED

***Conquering the vice of* acedia.** To practice hope, we must avoid the pitfalls of despair and presumption, as we have discussed. But despair goes by another name and in another form, and that is the sin of sloth or *acedia*. Despair and *acedia* are intimately linked, although they are distinct: "[T]he beginning and the root of despair is *acedia*, sloth."[16] The distinction is that despair is a hopelessness in future fulfillment, particularly in our redemption in Christ, whereas *acedia* "is a kind of sadness . . . more specifically, a sadness in view of the divine good in man. This sadness because of the God-given ennobling of human nature causes inactivity, depression, discouragement."[17] In other words, *acedia* is despair about our human potential given our status as creatures made in the image of God.

By design, humans are capable of grandeur, but we are also capable of turning that grandeur against God. Such is the story of the tower of Babel. We are capable of natural greatness (in science, art, politics, medicine, etc.) and spiritual greatness, through the work of the Holy Spirit and God's grace. Humans can grow in virtues and righteousness toward sanctification through the work of the Holy Spirit. That is how God designed us and preserves us. But sometimes this greatness is overwhelming, and instead of rising to what God has created us for in magnanimity, we fold in on ourselves, cower in fear, and hide in shame. Like a diver who hesitates at the edge of a diving board, we fear the greatness of our actions, so we freeze. And in that frozen state, we grow depressed and discouraged.

Pieper connects the specific form of depression that comes with *acedia* to the "worldly sorrow" Paul talks about in 2 Corinthians 7:10:

> This sorrow is a lack of magnanimity; it lacks courage for the great things that are proper to the nature of the Christian. It is a kind of anxious vertigo that befalls the human individual when he becomes aware of the height to which God has raised him. One who is trapped in *acedia* has neither the courage nor the will to be as great as he really is. He would prefer to be less great in order thus to avoid the obligation of greatness.[18]

The desire to be "less great" has the appearance of humility, but it is a *false* humility based on misunderstanding our right relationship to God. It actually *denies* our right relationship with God, which is forgiven, loved, and justified! And based on that justification we can walk in good works with boldness and courage.

Acedia is the depression which whispers into our ear that those truths are for other people, not us. That we are the exception. That we cannot turn from our sin. That we are too lost, too broken, too hopeless. That what is being asked of us by God is too great. And the concept of him loving us is too incomprehensible. We may intellectually understand it, but viscerally, and through our will, we deny God's love by punishing ourselves and neglecting God in prayer and the Word. At times we are tempted to abandon the faith altogether because at least then we wouldn't be "pretending" to be a Christian and we could embrace our worthlessness. These are the lies of *acedia*. Also known as the "noonday devil," it has troubled Christians for thousands of years. You are not alone.

The frozen state that often accompanies *acedia*, paradoxically, can appear as frantic busyness, so I don't want you to only picture someone who is stuck in bed depressed. In fact, many people try to submerge their *acedia* under constant work. Pieper ties workaholism to *acedia*![19] Through a thoroughly packed schedule we can avoid ourselves and the sadness of *acedia*, we can ignore the fact that we are created for good works which God designed beforehand that we may walk in them (Ephesians 2:10). Many modern people who anxiously work to improve their lives, master their bodies, and maximize their potential are actually working to escape the feeling of *acedia*, that they were created for God and can only find their fullness in him.

So how do we fight this "noonday devil"? How do we resist the power of *acedia* in our lives? Our tendency is to believe that we can busy our way out of sloth. But Pieper writes, "The opposite of *acedia* is not industry and diligence but magnanimity and that joy which is a fruit of the supernatural love of God."[20] It is in having the courage to be who God created us to be and resting in the joy of the Lord that we can overcome *acedia*, not in doing more activities. That magnanimity is rested on your *union with Christ*. The fact that you are in union with Christ means that you are justified, loved, and redeemed, a coheir with Christ, a beloved son and daughter of God. That is *who you are*. And this also gives us the *joy* Pieper speaks of, because when you remember the love you have received from God, you cannot help but feel joy in response.

Acedia involves a rejection of our status as children of God, but Pieper notes, "As a genuine possibility and necessity, however, this 'being a child of God' is an irrevocable fact that no one can alter."[21] We *are* children of God. That is an objective fact about the world. The real question is how we will *respond* to being a child of God. Will we magnanimously rise to the "upward call of God in Christ Jesus" (Philippians 3:14)? This requires a movement of our will, a decision to *act*, to pray like a child of God, even when you don't feel like a child of God. To read the Word as if it were written to *you*, because it was written to you, even though it may not feel like it at the time. And to venture out into the world to do good works for God's glory, even as the noon-day devil whispers in your ear that you are inadequate and a failure and should just stay in bed.

What's required to conquer *acedia* are the virtues of courage and hope. We want courage to live out our union with Christ by walking in righteousness and pursuing excellence (magnanimity) and we want hope in Christ's promises, to complete the good work he began in us, to preserve us, to keep us, to one day resurrect and glorify us, to accomplish all the good things Jesus prayed for us in that High Priestly Prayer. That hope anchors us and helps us see that the end is already written. *Acedia* is despair because it involves the surrender of all hope, the denial of our nature before God that leads to our eventual resurrection. Divine hope reminds us that our resurrection is secure, that God's love is secure, that we can strike out in freedom and courage, braving the day with confidence.

HOPING ALL THINGS: DESIRING THE GOOD OF THE OTHER

In Paul's famous list defining love (which we will address in the next chapter), he mentions that love "hopes all things" (1 Corinthians 13:7). This is a daunting task, if you think about it for any amount of time. To hope all things is to desire the good—God's good—for another person. It is usually easy to desire our own good or the good of those we love. I say "usually" because we regularly desire things that are actually harmful to us, or good things in harmful amounts. But on the whole, we desire good things: to get a good job, to see our children stay healthy, that our friends would have pleasant lives, and so on.

The difficult thing, but the very thing required of us by love, is to hope for the good of others who are not like us, or who are hostile to us, or who harm us, or who are our enemies. Hope here means to bend our will, particularly in prayer, but also in action when applicable, toward good future fulfillment for someone. You may be wondering why you would want to desire "good future fulfillment" for your enemies, which is a fair question, but it hinges on our understanding of the concept of *good*. As I said before, *good* here is defined by God, which means to desire the good of your enemies is not to desire them to prosper in doing evil, but to repent and pursue righteousness!

Applied to politics, to hope all things does not require us to abandon "reality," but it does demand that we desire a good outcome that goes beyond likely outcomes. For example, I ought to desire (hope) that the Democratic Party will adopt a pro-life platform despite knowing that such an adoption is unlikely. So when I hear of a pro-life Democrat, instead of scoffing at their inconsistency with the rest of the party, I rejoice that they are not supporting abortion! I ought to desire that certain leaders of the Republican Party start treating third-world immigrants with dignity even when their track record shows that it's unlikely. And when I see signs of them speaking of immigrants with dignity, I rejoice rather than scoff cynically, because it's good for our leaders to treat people with dignity!

My job is not to focus on likelihood but what is good. I don't put my hope in the major political parties reforming into virtuous institutions; my hope is in Christ and his second coming. But I hope *for* and work *toward* change. The alternative is resignation, a hopeless belief that nothing will ever improve, that *those people* will always be terrible, that we might as well write them off as lost causes.

Much of our social life (including politics) is determined by our expectations, our hope or lack of hope. When you have no hope that your roommate will change their ways and help with the household chores, you begin acting and speaking in ways that reinforce their bad habits. You do the chores yourself and never bother to ask them to help. It may be that you have good historic reasons for having no expectations that they will participate in the upkeep of the house, but by choosing to be resigned to that norm, you excuse and condone their neglect.

To hope all things is to desire the good for your roommate. And the good doesn't mean a more comfortable life for them, where they are not asked to help. The good involves them participating fully in the life of the household. To hope all things is to invite them into the work of the house, to ask them to participate, to *expect* them to help. Resignation is the opposite of hope. When we are resigned, we desire things to get worse or stay bad while simultaneously feeling frustrated that they don't improve, so we suffer twice.

The same dynamic is at work in our politics. We resign ourselves to corrupt, immoral (or at best amoral), deceitful politicians even while we complain about how corrupt, immoral, and deceitful they are. We never ask or demand honesty from them, because we don't hope all things. And this is doubly true when it comes to the opposing political party. *Those* people are always corrupt, immoral, and deceitful, and there's nothing we can do about that except defeat them politically. No thought is given to the possibility that a political party might mature in their platform and repent of their support for evil. In a perverse way, we *desire them* to remain evil because we wouldn't know what to do with ourselves if they changed. A failure to hope all things creates perverse incentives for people to desire the moral corruption of those with whom we find ourselves in conflict, whether that is in our personal or political lives.

Of course, hoping all things is costly because you will be disappointed. When you hope for your loved one to turn from their life of addiction and substance abuse, they will likely let you down. For the Christian, our ultimate hope is in Christ and his work of making all things new, which gives us the freedom to hope for people to change without placing our happiness or even contentment on their choices.

Hoping all things is not just another way of assuming the best of someone. Hoping all things involves a desire for good, not an assumption that the good will take place. You can be a hopeful realist: desiring the good for your neighbor while accepting the likelihood that they will pursue an evil path for themselves and others. From a worldly perspective, hoping all things is dangerous and irrational. The most optimal perspective is to identify and hedge on the most likely outcome, whatever that may be. To hope all things is to desire the good of someone regardless of the probability of that good occurring while trusting in God that he will accomplish his will.

CONCLUSION

In T. S. Eliot's *Four Quartets*, specifically the section titled "Little Gidding," Eliot offers this reflection on hope and despair:

> The only hope, or else despair
> Lies in the choice of pyre or pyre—
> To be redeemed from fire by fire.[22]

For all of us, our only hope, lies in a choice of "pyre or pyre." The alternative is "despair," and we have seen what despair does to us. We must all go through the burning experience of life, the purgatorial fires of purification. Whether you reject the concept of purgatory, as I do, or not, the concept of the Christian life as a sanctifying fire has its basis in Scripture (1 Corinthians 3:13).

Our hope for redemption comes through the Holy Spirit's work in purifying us as if by fire, cleansing us of our sins, cultivating in us the fruits of the Spirit, burning away all that is ungodly. Eliot's intention is to brace us for the reality of hope. Real hope demands courage. It demands more than natural courage; it requires supernatural courage from the Holy Spirit to allow us to endure. Our hope goes through the momentary suffering of this life, including the suffering of waiting for fulfillment, for the One who suffered on our behalf.

Our culture will continue to pull us to the twin vices of presumption and despair. *Technique* will continue to promise us that fulfillment has come or is just around the corner if we just live long enough. Certain secular justice activists will continue to despair that reconciliation and justice are achievable. And a million other despair panderers will sell their wares in the form of addictions, distractions, and memes. For the Christian, the virtue of hope allows us to rise above the false hope of techno-optimists and all those who presume to have achieved a fulfilled ultimate hope and reject the allure of despair in all its forms. But as Eliot reminds us, hope takes courage, the courage to endure the long wait for the "not yet" fulfillment which is coming. Christ is coming, and he will make all things right. As Eliot says elsewhere in *Four Quartets*, "the faith and the love and the hope are all in the waiting."[23]

7

LOVING RIGHTLY

NOW WE TURN TO WHAT the apostle Paul called the greatest of all virtues, love. Unfortunately, this virtue has been confused in modern society, yet another piece of the "heap of broken images"[1] that we live with. In truth, "love" has always been misunderstood to some extent by different cultures and times. Today love excuses and justifies a multitude of sins. It is love to allow people to live however they choose, no matter how much that choice deviates from God's creational design, his law, and their own good. It's not only love to legally permit same-sex marriages and gender transitions; to fully love, according to contemporary theory of the virtue, requires us to approve, affirm, and celebrate such choices publicly. The very idea that it might be immoral and destructive to be in a sexual relationship outside of a married, heterosexual couple seems not only prudish but blasphemous.

The god we are blaspheming here is the god of Autonomy. Love, to our culture, is an intensely personal experience and an expression of an emotion. Love is love, we are told. We are also told that "love wins," but whose love, and in what way? Well, since this love is an "intensely personal experience," the love that wins has to be private, incommunicable, and inarguable. It just *is*. And there can be no challenging it.

This is a theory of love predicated upon the idea that we are each our own and belong to ourselves. It is love for the sovereign individual. If we belong to ourselves, then love is a personal expression of inward desire toward whatever object or objects resonate with us. We are at the mercies of our loves. They are what they are. The heart will love what it loves. All we can do is choose to live authentically to that love. Because love is tied up with the very center of our sovereign selves, of who we are as free agents in the world, it is sacred and precious.

And in expressing my love, I become myself, I express my identity to the world. I become a full self when I allow my inner love to be expressed. This is a form of expressive individualism, the belief that we gain an identity by looking inward and expressing ourselves to the world, constantly. As I have written about in previous books, it is the predominant conception of the self in the contemporary West.

There can be no boundaries on our love, because there are no boundaries on the self—only the most necessary boundaries for legal protections against those who cannot voice proper consent: children and animals. The very idea that there could be good and bad objects of love is incoherent to the modern ear. If you accept that we are our own, a freedom to love whomever and whatever you wish makes perfect sense. But it also leaves us naturally in chaos, emotionally and socially, since we were not designed to create and shatter loves at the whim of our inner self.

I'm reminded once again of Charles Taylor's perceptive remark, "For many people today, to set aside their own path in order to conform to some external authority just doesn't seem comprehensible as a form of spiritual life."[2] This is especially true when it comes to matters of love. How could it be a spiritual act to deny the innermost expression of love which I discover inside myself, even if that expression calls for me to abandon my wife and children? As Taylor observes, for many people such a spiritual conception of love is incomprehensible. It puts limits on two of the most sacred things to the modern person: the inner self and love, which are all but synonymous.

Love in this sense is the most powerful and empty term in the modern language. It can be used to justify any act of neglect or sin, and yet it still carries with it the indelible weight of its original meanings, which is why appeals to love have so much power. Regardless of how flippantly people might use the word "love," we all instinctively know its rich meaning. We might struggle with the full meaning of love because of the way we have misused it and misapplied it, but we have a sense, particularly if we have had the privilege of healthy parental bonding, of the affirming gaze which says to us, "You are safe, you are good, you are mine." Love is built into the fabric of creation, which only makes it easier to misuse and to abuse.

A not insignificant part of the confusion of love in the modern world is the reduction of all love into sexual or romantic love. We see this clearly in the crisis of male friendships in America today. After decades of insinuating that straight men who loved their male friends were secretly queer (e.g., "Were Jonathan and David queer lovers because they 'loved' each other?"), we shouldn't be surprised by the trepidation some men feel to express their affection toward each other. The oversexualization of our culture has reduced love to an ever-narrower range. Increasingly we seem to be only capable of sexual love and loving our pets. Children and the elderly are tolerated in fewer social spaces and there is less and less communal feeling of love for them. When love is reduced to sex, it becomes atrophied, and whole swaths of human experience are denied to us.

Once we begin from the premises that we are our own and belong to ourselves and expressive individualism (which go hand in hand), then "loving someone" will naturally come to mean something like "affirming the expression of identity of another." And "loving things" will naturally come to mean something like "this feels pleasurable to me." But as we will discover, both of these expressions are hollow. They are mere shadows of true love that fail to capture the wonder and beauty and richness of the divine experience. Practicing the virtue of love in the contemporary world is difficult because the definition of love has been so polluted by our distorted anthropology. Our conception of who we are as people is wrong, so our conception of love is wrong. And it begins with the fact that we were created.

LOVE DEFINED

There can be no better image of love in human history than Christ's sacrifice on the cross for our sins. Not just the sacrifice itself, but the long build-up. The moment in the garden, which we have already discussed as a moment of fortitude, and the trial, the beating, the humiliation and degradation. All for our sakes. Yet despite all these agonies and sufferings, and the horrors of the cross itself, Jesus looked up from his place of torment and prayed, "Father, forgive them, for they know not what they do" (Luke 23:34). Such a heart of mercy could only come from a love for people as precious creatures made in the image of God, the heart of a God who wishes that none should perish "but that all should reach repentance" (2 Peter 3:9). Christ himself identified his death as the greatest form of love when he said, "Greater love has no one than this, that someone lay down his life for his friends" (John 15:13). Love is an affirmation of the existence of someone or something that is willing to sacrifice for the goodness of that love.

The first place we should look to define "love" is 1 Corinthians chapter 13 where the apostle Paul gives his famous discourse on love:

> Love is patient and kind; love does not envy or boast; it is not arrogant or rude. It does not insist on its own way; it is not irritable or resentful; it does not rejoice at wrongdoing, but rejoices with the truth. Love bears all things, believes all things, hopes all things, endures all things. (1 Corinthians 13:4-7)

While these verses give us a firm grasp of the characteristics of love, they don't quite define love as a phenomenon. They tell us how love should behave, but not what love means. Whatever "love" is, we know it must adhere to this description in 1 Corinthians 13. Love is no less than patient, kind, free from envy and boasting, and so on, but is it more than these qualities? In Pieper's masterful essay on love, he explores various definitions from philosophers before coming to his own conclusion.

Pieper's definition of love is simple and yet powerful, and is grounded in creation itself: "[L]oving someone or something means finding him or it *probs*, the Latin word for 'good.' It is a way of turning to him or it and saying, 'It's good that you exist; it's good that you are in this world!'"[3] Unlike contemporary love which says, "It's good that you are this or that (identity)," true love affirms the *very existence* of the person in the world. Identity is trivial, ephemeral, compared to their being.

Pieper goes on to connect this love to creation: "Human love, therefore, is by its nature and must inevitably be always an imitation and a kind of repetition of this perfected and, in the exact sense of the word, *creative* love of God."[4] Just as God called his creation "good," so we affirm the creative goodness of people around us, who are likewise made in the image of God. Every moment of the day, God chooses to preserve and sustain this person before you in an act of creative love, and so when we tell that person we love them, we are merely echoing God's affirmation of love!

This definition of love fits with the list of qualities of love given by Paul in 1 Corinthians. When you recognize the goodness of someone's existence as created by God, you naturally should desire to be patient and kind with them, to not envy them or boast, and so on. Paul's list in 1 Corinthians is not an alternative definition of love, but a description of the qualities of love that flow naturally from affirming God's creative act for this person.

Understood this way, love is less an emotion than an act of the will, something we choose intentionally. This is another way the contemporary view of love has confused us, with its overly emotive view of love. When we love someone or something by affirming them, we make a conscious choice. Rather than wait for some emotion to well up inside of us, we look on them and *choose* to delight in the goodness of their being. This does not come from a place of neutrality.[5] You will be naturally drawn toward some people and some things, but you have a choice of what to do with your loves, how to express them, how to develop them, and how to order them. Here we can see a great divergence from the contemporary vision of love as an uncontrollable force inside us which we must obey.

When we define love as affirming someone, this is not assent to the lifestyle of the person, but their existence, their presence in the world. This affirmation also includes a desire for their moral good, for them to live righteously. Pieper addresses the question many of you might be asking: "I would first of all suggest that 'exist' signifies, not a purely static being-there, but something that is in process and that 'continues.' And of course the lover wishes it to continue *well*."[6] If you love someone, you will desire their good, whether they perceive it as good or not. To do otherwise is a failure of love (and of hope!). We accept this intuitively when it comes to drug addicts and alcoholics who are slowly killing themselves through addictions, but outside of these extreme cases, our society is hesitant to judge for other people what their good is.

To love someone is to desire their good, their ultimate good. Not what the individual envisions as the good, but what is objectively the good. And *the* good is always union with Christ. The good is always growing into fullness of our nature, and our nature is to be in communion with God. The good is always becoming our full humanity, which involves the cultivation of virtues. Granted, we often do not know the *particulars* of the good for any one person. Does the good entail taking a particular job or watching a specific film or wearing certain clothes? Who is to say?

But we do know the *contours* of the good. We know that it always necessarily culminates in a vision of and union with Christ, and that this good is achieved by grace through faith. We know that the fruit of that faith is righteous living before a God who is present and cares about our actions in this life. So, to love someone is to desire that they live in communion with God, in union with Christ, on a path of self-denial and growth in the virtues.

If love means affirming the existence of someone, ultimate love is affirming their existence in light of their design. That existence is not without an end. Everyone has a *telos* they were created for, a purpose, a direction built into the very fabric of their being in the world. For each of us, our existence, the thing we love when we love, is bent toward the glorification of God, which is why when we love someone and affirm their existence, the thing we affirm is the person as they were created to be, not the person as they self-created themselves. Here we can see that true love requires another divergence from the contemporary understanding of love.

This is not to say that we are to love an *imagined* person, the person we desire them to be. For example, sometimes in a romantic relationship, one person will dangerously overlook flaws that ought to be addressed in the other person because they choose to love an imagined person who is more ideal. I describe this as dangerous because it is a failure of *prudence* to see reality rightly. This is not the same thing as choosing to love who they were created to be. When you love someone for who they were created to be, you are loving them for their *real*, current nature, as someone made for union with God, not for some *imagined* state.

To explore the challenge of loving someone who is fallen—a challenge all of us must face—Pieper acknowledges that there are two main categories: weaknesses and guilt.[7] With weaknesses, which are minor flaws in a person's character or behavior, we learn to love the person "*in spite*" of the weaknesses, while never approving of or loving the "weaknesses themselves."[8] Guilt is another matter entirely. Guilt is sin and must be dealt with. We tend to deal with guilt in two ways, Pieper says: We excuse it or we forgive it.

On the whole, our culture prefers us to excuse sin: "By 'excusing' we mean discounting what is bad. We 'let it be' although it is bad; we ignore the evil; we don't care; we are indifferent to it; we don't worry about it."[9] But when we love someone, we can't excuse guilt by discounting what is bad. That is not loving to the person and that is not honoring to God. We cannot ignore what is evil: "Now there is very little if anything that a lover should 'excuse' in the above sense—whereas he can forgive the beloved *everything*."[10]

Forgiveness is very different from excusing. It desires the loved one to repent and mature in Christ for their own good, and it holds them accountable for their actions. Our model of forgiveness in love comes from God, who first loved and forgave us and commanded us to likewise forgive others (Matthew 6:14-15). Where there has been harm done in relationships, trust may be broken and have to be earned back, healthy boundaries may need to be established, and there may be other natural consequences, but *forgiveness* happens.

When no repentance is shown or forgiveness sought, love becomes a burden. The other's existence is a strain on you, a reminder of a rupture and the broken nature of your relationship. It is precisely *because* the other's existence is a miracle that it hurts that they would betray you. To love the other's existence in this moment is to desire that they repent, for even as you carry around the burden of a severed relationship, they carry around the burden of their sin. And that is a heavy burden, the burden of an unreconciled relationship.

We should still choose to forgive them of their sins, which may be very difficult depending on the offense, because Christ calls us to forgive our neighbor (Matthew 6:14-15) and because to hold on to an offense will leave us bitter and wounded. But this does not mean we are *reconciled* until they have repented and made restitution. Depending on the situation, it may be necessary to bring in the church and apply the prescription given by Christ in Matthew 18:15-17 for dealing with a brother or sister in sin. But sometimes those who sin against us are not in the church, and we must learn to love them even when they don't seek forgiveness for the harm they have caused us. In these situations, the best we can do is lovingly set healthy boundaries so that we are not senselessly harmed again, especially while we continue to hope, pray, and desire for them to repent.

If love does not excuse evil, then how are we to love people in a fallen world who are so immersed in evil? I think Pieper gives us some good examples in his explanation of "excusing." Let's look at that again: "By 'excusing' we mean discounting what is bad. We 'let it be' although it is bad; we ignore the evil; we don't care; we are indifferent to it; we don't worry about it."[11] When we have people in our lives who are close to us and are choosing to live in sin, it is worth asking ourselves, are we discounting what is bad in their lives? Saying to ourselves, "Oh, I know it's not *right*, but he could be into much worse things." Or do we "let it be" and "ignore the evil" by not ever addressing it? Or do we not "care" or "worry about it"? Do we devote any time to praying for the person and their sin? Do we *hope all things* for the person we love or have we resigned ourselves in despair to their sin?

When you love someone, your impulse is to want to make life easier for them, and so to confront them with their sin, or even to acknowledge that there might be a better, more righteous way to live can feel like you are failing to love. But that's backward thinking: "[T]o love a person does not mean to wish him to live free of all burdens. It means, rather, to wish that everything associated with him may truly be good."[12] Part of the definition of love is being willing to burden your loved ones with what will bring them to healing, righteousness, and God. What a strange description of love to modern ears: Love means being willing to burden someone for their own good!

When we affirm the existence of another, the primary thing we're affirming is not their character traits, but their existence as created by God. As Pieper says, "For what the lover gazing upon his beloved says and means is *not*: How good that you are *so* (so clever, useful, capable, skillful), but: It's good that you are; how wonderful that you exist!"[13] Of course you still find those positive qualities attractive, but that is not what you *love* about the person. And this is important because most qualities change with time. Beauty fades. Usefulness runs out. Cleverness dulls. Skills grow clumsy. Yet love remains. Why? Because what you loved in that person was not their beauty, usefulness, cleverness, or skills, but their very being, what Pieper calls their "core" self, which appears more and more to a lover over time.[14]

For some of us, there is a deep anxiety about being loved. We feel unworthy to be an object of affirmation, and the desire to be loved feels self-centered and selfish. In Pieper's view, the desire for human love is not only natural and good, but something that "in a certain sense [is] even a perfecting of what was begun in the course of creation."[15] There are some biblical grounds for this in Genesis 2:18 when God says, "It is not good that the man should be alone." Like Adam, we all have a longing for human love even though we have a relationship of divine love with God.

Whether it is through a spouse or a friend, the gaze of affirmation from another human being seems to be essential to human flourishing: "[M]an succeeds in fully 'existing' and feeling at home in the world only when he is 'being confirmed' by the love of another."[16] It is natural and good to love and to long for love. It is part of the created order. And this means that there is nothing inherently selfish or sinful about desiring love or to be loved. Sometimes, as Pieper notes throughout his essay on love, Christians seek after a desireless love—a love that has no expectations and no longings, an entirely disinterested and selfless love, which sounds very nice on the surface—but in reality, we were made to desire love. Most significantly, we were created to desire and delight in God's love. There is absolutely nothing selfish or sinful about desiring and enjoying the love of God.

Similarly, there is nothing necessarily selfish or sinful about desiring and enjoying the love of your spouse, so long as that love does not become disordered. The love becomes disordered when it prioritizes its own good above God and the good of the spouse and other members of the family. Then it will inevitably become abusive, coercive, and sterile. There will be no joy in love, only power. When a husband loves his own good over the good of his wife, he may grow bitter when his sexual desires are not fulfilled. When a wife loves her own good over the good of her husband, she may grow critical when he does not meet her expectations. But if you are delighting in the love of your spouse and you desire that delight *as a gift from God*, that is a good and proper thing.

Of course, you will also desire love for the sake of your beloved; no true love for a person can be entirely for its own sake. But neither does love require you to deny your desire for the pure joy of love. A key here is gratitude. Pieper's definition of love is the affirmation, "It's good that you exist; it's good that you are in this world!"[17] Implied in that affirmation is gratitude to the Creator who made the world and the person whom we love. Gratitude helps keep us from turning righteous desiring love to sinful, selfish, possessive love.

Not only is it appropriate for our love to be interested and desiring for our sake as well as for the sake of the beloved, it is also appropriate and good for us to love ourselves. I know this is a difficult concept for many to accept. Some have been told too many times by self-help gurus to "love yourself" in vapid, quasi-therapeutic ways so that the phrase makes us feel a little ill. Others have internalized so much self-criticism and loathing that the thought of loving themselves feels impossible. Still others believe that the doctrine of total depravity requires us to hate ourselves. I resonate with all of these reasons, and yet they are all wrong.

First John 4:19 tells us, "We love because he first loved us," which means that the basis for all our love is God's original act of loving us. All our acts of love, *all of them*, stem from his original gesture of love. This is true of everyone, not just Christians. Even those who don't believe in God can only love because God loved them enough to create the world and them in it. Out of God's original act of love, the first person we love is ourselves.

The Bible assumes that we love ourselves, as stated in the second great commandment in Mark 12:31: "You shall love your neighbor as yourself." Saint Augustine argued, "If you don't know how to love yourself, how will you be able to love your neighbor in truth?"[18] Love of self is fundamental to life and is an echo of God's original and ongoing love of us. We don't love ourselves because we are self-centered creatures. We love ourselves because "He first loved us."

Because of that we have an obligation to care for ourselves, our bodies and minds, and it is that care, attention, and desire for good that gives us the model for *how to love our neighbor*. We were created to seek our own happiness in God, which is a form of self-love, argues Pieper.[19] In self-love, we affirm our own being in the world, which God has created and sustained in love. We say to ourselves, "It is *good* that you exist! How wonderful that you are!"[20]

Our love for ourselves never excuses or justifies sin, but it is kind, patient, encouraging, and magnanimous. By magnanimous I mean that our love for ourselves sees the goal as reaching our full potential as a human made in the image of God. Anything less than that is a failure to truly affirm our existence. Put differently, your "is" has an inherent "ought." The fact that you exist points you toward some end, some purpose. Self-love does not overlook our sin nature but sees our sin nature as God sees it.

That's a terrifying and comforting thought, but so is love. We see our sins as the horrors they are, but we also see them as fully paid for by the blood of Jesus. That is precisely how God sees me, and so he can love us without neglecting or excusing our sins. And he desires that we grow and mature despite our fallenness. Hoping all things for us, desiring all good things for us. Even so, we must hope all things for ourselves, desire all good things for ourselves. Not out of selfish conceit, but as an echo of God's original love.

Love requires us to cultivate all the other virtues. To love someone involves having the prudence to know how to meaningfully affirm their existence. What does it look like to recognize their unique otherness and affirm it through acts of kindness? That requires prudence. Justice sets the baseline for love. To love someone is to act justly toward them, to give them their due and then some. Love requires a great deal of fortitude, for it is courageous to love someone in a world of suffering and heartbreak. Any act of love involves the risk of rejection and loss. At some point each of us will face the loss of those we love, but we must have the courage to love anyway.

With temperance, we learn to love the right things to the right extent and in the right manner. Love should have a balance and a proper sense of proportion, particularly because we are called to love so many people in this life. If we did not love proportionately, we would not do justice to everyone. But true love requires faith, the faith to know that all love flows rightly from God, from the fact that he first loved us. That is the foundation for all our loves. The more we rightly understand God's love for us, the more we can share that love with others. Finally, love hopes all things, as we have discussed. Love demands that we hope good of the beloved.

But love is also the key to all the other virtues. Without love, we cannot see reality accurately in order to make prudent decisions. Without love, justice becomes rigid and inhuman. Without love, fortitude cannot rightly identify the good and pursue it through suffering. Without love, we cannot rightly order our lives according to the good. Without love, our faith in Christ will grow cold. And without love, our hope in the resurrection becomes a hollow, mechanistic theology that cannot sustain us through times of trial. Love is at the center of all virtues.

LOVE APPLIED

Attention. Love requires attention. This is especially important to keep in mind in our attention economy in which technology and entertainment tries to gobble up all our attention. Everything is vying for our attention, and what we choose to give our attention to, we choose to give our lives to. Love means paying attention. One of the most precious goods you possess in life is time, and most of that time exists internally: the time we spend thinking about something or someone.

It is worth asking ourselves, who or what do we attend to with our thoughts? What fills our mind? In other words, where do the eyes of our mind gaze? Do they look to God, or our spouse or friends or loved ones or a neighbor, or are they distracted with the noise of the world? In your quiet moments, you have the power to choose what to think about, what to attend to, and that choice reflects what and who you love.

The choice to attend to someone before you is a great act of love. You are giving your life (measured in time) to this person. This is why it is so powerful when someone looks you in the eyes when they are talking to you. In that moment you *feel* their attention on you. You know that they are giving you a piece of their life, even while everything and everyone else demands their attention, they are putting their gaze on you. In that moment you feel like the absolute center of the universe.

Normally, to "feel like the center of the universe" is a bad thing, a feeling of judgment, but in love attention makes you aware of the goodness of your existence. They are gazing on you because your very existence is a beautiful gift. They are so glad that you exist that they will use up part of their life directing their attention toward your being in the world. How wonderful is that? The ideal form of love is God's gaze upon us. His gaze is perfect. He never turns his face from us, he sees us perfectly, and he affirms our existence fully because when he looks on us he sees the righteousness of his Son. All human gazes of love are shadows of his loving gaze.

This desire to be affirmed through a loving gaze explains why some people seek attention at any cost, even negative attention. If I can make you look at me, even in disgust, you are acknowledging my reality by sacrificing your attention. I feel seen and known and therefore affirmed. But real affirmation comes from the affirmation of our being, not the acknowledgment that we exist. There is a significant difference, although often we obscure it.

There is a sleight of hand at work that allows one to substitute the affirmation of our being for the acknowledgment of our being. The latter is the mere fact about reality without any approval. The former is the claim that it is good that we exist. One is scientific observation, the other is love. But when you are lonely enough, even a scientific observation can take the place of love. People commit terrible crimes and acts of violence and drama to gain negative attention so that they feel seen and therefore alive. We all rightly desire the gaze of love, but we don't always rightly pursue it.

If the meaning of love is the affirmation that it is good that the beloved exists, then the highest form of love is sacrifice of your life for the life of another. Christ's sacrifice on the cross is our model of sacrificial love, as we have seen, but sacrificial love doesn't always mean a literal dying for someone, although it certainly can be that. There are little ways we die to ourselves for the sake of others. At the most basic level, giving attention to someone else is a form of sacrifice. You have a limited amount of time on this earth, and whatever you choose to give your eyes to, that is what you love. A gaze is a practice of love as a practice of sacrifice. Spending time with someone. Listening to someone attentively. All these are acts of sacrifice that embody love by affirming the existence of another.

We practice loving others by choosing wisely what to give our attention to. When we sit and listen attentively to a friend who is struggling, we are loving them. When we attend to an elderly neighbor's lawn for them, we are loving them. When we put our phones away during dinner and talk with our friends or family, we are loving them. When you attend to the needs of your spouse rather than insisting on your own way, you are loving them. We love what we give our attention to, and I'm afraid we tend to give our attention to the wrong things and for the wrong reasons. The reality of our time is that there are individuals at major corporations whose job it is to get us addicted to smartphone games, social media platforms, apps, pornography, the headlines—anything that will capture our attention. They are stealing our love away from better things. To practice the virtue of love in the contemporary world means fighting to keep your attention focused on what is worthy of your love.

Friendship. We don't tell our friends we love them enough. Maybe because we don't love them. Maybe because we don't open ourselves up to the hurt of real, loving friendships. True friendship, like any meaningful form of love, involves the risk of great heartbreak, the risk that they will betray your trust, the risk that they will hurt you, the risk that they will abandon you. Even if they are trustworthy, kind, loving friends, there is always the heartbreak of empathy, which grows so deep in close friendships. When your friend suffers through a difficult time, the more you love them, the more you will feel their suffering.

The efficient thing to do is to maximize the aspects of friendships that have utility (someone to do things with, someone to help you move, social networking, etc.) and pleasure (someone to have a good laugh with) while minimizing the aspects of friendships that involve high risk (being vulnerable, relying on someone, being someone's support system). This roughly aligns with Aristotle's three types of friendship: utility, pleasure, and what he believed to be the ideal form of friendship, virtue. It's risky to develop friendships of virtue, which are defined by a desire for the good, a desire for God.[21] They take time and honesty.

It feels like modern life has done this to us, made us make these kinds of calculations so that we distance ourselves from people who could really know us and love us. Our jobs encourage us to build friendships of utility with coworkers, but they also want us to be flexible about where we live and the hours we work. Technology gives us ever-increasing ways to connect with people, but also makes us lazy and less inclined to meet with friends in person, where love can most unrestrainedly be conveyed.

And yet, we need friends whom we can love more than ever, because the world is hostile, violent, corrosive, and cruel. We need people we can call at any moment when we're having a mental breakdown. We need people who will love us despite our sins and failings. We need people who will walk with us through tragedy and trauma—and not just the interesting kinds of tragedy. I mean the ugly, earthly, mundane, disgusting tragedies of everyday life.

We need people who will disagree with us politically and love us just the same, not an ounce less. We were created for friendship, and we know this. As Aristotle wrote, "[N]o one would choose to live without friends even if he had all the other goods."[22] And yet, according to C. S. Lewis, "[F]ew value [friendship] because few experience it," and I suspect this is particularly true in the modern world.[23]

Realistically, close, virtuous friendships do not just *happen* to us. They must be intentionally cultivated over time. Especially as you age, friendships become harder and harder to cultivate. Work, children, obligations, and urban sprawl make it difficult to sacrifice the time to be with someone else. Just as in romantic love, so in friendship, we show our love for someone by sacrificing moments of our lives to be with that person. We give them ourselves, and join in their adventure of life, uniting ourselves with them, which is very difficult to do when your job insists that you work after hours answering emails or finishing projects, or when you are busy shuttling kids from various club sporting events. Combine these forces pulling us apart with the rise in autonomy and independence, and you have the perfect storm for an epidemic of loneliness, which is precisely what we have according to the Surgeon General.[24] Many adult men have no close friends.[25] How can you survive this life without friends bearing you up?

C. S. Lewis, in his beautiful book *The Four Loves*, argues that the love between friends appears as two people standing side-by-side staring at and loving the same thing.[26] Picture two men watching a basketball game together. Some of my most meaningful conversations have taken place while I sat and watched a game with a friend. Or it might look like taking a walk with someone and enjoying the air and creation. Or it might look like two women crocheting together while they listen to music and sip tea. Or running together. Driving together. Making music together.

Whatever it is, the crucial point here is in loving the same thing at the same time, standing side-by-side gazing at a beloved object. As we explored in our discussion of prudence, we "love to know," using Esther Meek's language, and it's also true that we know to love. It is a cyclical process. As we love something with someone else, we come to know that thing and that person better. It may be that you love a local church and work to serve it with a friend. As you sacrifice time and effort and money to care for that local congregation, you learn more about the needs, the spiritual weaknesses and strengths, the hurt and the joy of that congregation, but also those of your friend. By working in love side-by-side with them, you come to know them better.

But all of this assumes something fundamental: You must love something. In order to stand next to a friend and love the same object, you must have *something that you truly love*. If you are indifferent to everything, aloof, or stoic, you will not have anything to give yourself to with someone else, which means that if you find yourself friendless, the first step to gaining friends is to find something to love and find others that love that thing too. Love a sport, gardening, running, cycling, history, literature, serving a community, dancing, coaching youth sports—find and love something. The person without friends would do well to examine whether they have any true loves in their life and to ask whether those loves could be shared by those around them.

For deep friendships to take root, you must practice giving attention and sacrificing time. Deep friendships require years of walking through life together with someone, attending to them as they experience joy and sorrow and face challenges and opportunities. As you listen to them and learn their story, you must learn to be vulnerable and share your story too. You will have to sacrifice and make time to meet with them, and not just for "events," but for unscheduled leisure: meals or coffee with no agenda, for example. It is during these aimless times of being with someone that you are able to learn about them, where you will feel comfortable opening up, where random conversations will lead you places you didn't expect. The mystery of another person appears in leisure.

One mistake people make about friendship is in assuming that a close friend must share your political or theological views. Naturally it's nice when someone thinks like you, but as Proverbs 27:17 tells us, there is value in iron sharpening iron. All my closest friendships have been with men who I have disagreements with to some degree. Sometimes those disagreements are explicit, and we discuss them, sometimes they are acknowledged and unspoken. We agree to disagree. I could hunt for people who better align with my personal views. They exist. But I would be very lonely and sad if I did. I believe I am a wiser man because my friends have challenged me. Love does not require similarity; it requires affirmation, and not affirmation of your *views*, but of your existence. I affirm the personhood of my friends even as I reject some of their views. As a Christian, I have developed friendships with those who disagree with me on a variety of issues but who share a deep love of Christ. Despite our differences, we can stand together and gaze at Christ.

In my experience, the great gift of friendship is the wisdom and support that will help you through life's many complexities and troubles. I believe this is true for all of us, whether married or single. It's true that in marriage husbands and wives have each other as helpmates, but practically, life demands more than what any spouse can bear. Everyone needs friends. Love allows the close friend to admonish you when you have wandered into sin. Love allows the close friend to speak honest and insightful words of encouragement to you when your mind plagues you with self-doubt. Love allows the close friend to preach the gospel to you when you deny it in your despair. Love allows the close friend to invite you to minister to them in their need. Love allows the close friend to remind you of the joy of beauty in God's creation. The love of a close friend reminds you of the original love of God, which is its purpose.

In many ways I fear we have professionalized the roles of friendships, handing over wise counsel exclusively to the realm of therapy. While there is certainly room for therapy, there is also room for the wise counsel of loving friends. When we cultivate close friendships, we allow ourselves to participate in the intimate lives of others and allow them to participate in ours, gaining wisdom and prudence in how to love our neighbors and serve the Lord. Of course, this involves a great measure of *vulnerability*, but as we saw with the virtue of fortitude, vulnerability is necessary in life. You can't be courageous if you are not first vulnerable! The love of a good friend requires us to be vulnerable with them, allowing them to affirm our existence as good and understand the mystery of our existence as they come to know us. We must have courage to make friends, the endurance to be with them through challenging times, and the love to sacrifice for them. But it's worth it. The gift of friendship is one of the greatest gifts God has given us in this life.

Love of God. All love comes down to the love of the Creator of all love, the source of all love, love himself. When we love God rightly, we have hope for tomorrow, our faith is deepened and sustained with truth, we naturally moderate our desires according to the good, we have the courage to endure suffering, we advocate for the justice of our neighbor and ourselves, and we have the prudence to choose wisely. The center of our being, of our movement in the world, is the love God has for us, which we are called to reflect back to him in a circle of mutuality.

As we experience the love of God more deeply, we are capable of loving God more in return. Our love of God is the declaration that it is good that he exists. He exists whether or not we affirm the goodness of his being, but our affirmation includes the affirmation of all his being entails. By affirming his existence, we affirm his justice, righteousness, long-suffering, grace, creation, mercy, power—all aspects of his nature.

Practically, we love God by loving his creation moment by moment and delighting in it as he would have us delight in it. By that I mean that we participate in this life righteously, moderated by temperance, justice, and prudence. Loving God is the constant awareness that you are not radically autonomous but radically dependent on God for everything good. Christ taught us that if we love him, we are to keep his commandments (John 14:15). Love overflows into action. Recall that for Pieper, love is an orientation of the will. Here Christ commands us to orient our will in line with his will, which is for our good! In loving God, we keep his commandments and delight in his creation in gratitude and for his and our own good.

We may not always or even often *feel* a love for God. Feelings are fleeting. I think for many of us, it is difficult to feel a certain way toward a being whom we cannot see or touch. We struggle to have a deeply emotional response to God. Of course many other people have profound emotional responses to God, but that makes those of us who are less emotive feel broken, as if our spiritual lives are stunted. But if love is primarily a matter of the will, not the emotion, then what matters most is what you choose to do with your love, not how you feel when singing a worship song any given Sunday. Will you choose to sing, as Paul commands us (Ephesians 5:19)? Will you choose to gather for worship, as the author of Hebrews commands us (Hebrews 10:25)? Will you choose to sacrifice your wandering attention and confess your sins earnestly?

Some days I feel God's love for me; some days I feel the accusations of the devil condemning me for my sins or failings, persuading me that there is no love, only judgment or indifference. But as with my love for God, God's love for me is not based on my feelings or intrusive thoughts. God's love is based on Christ's objective work of sacrificial love on the cross for my sins, so there is no condemnation in Christ (Romans 8:1). His love is outside of my head and my logic of condemnation and despair. No matter how persuasive my own case for self-condemnation is, his case for justification is infinitely greater, which means that when I don't feel the love of God, my duty is to *act* on the love of God. I need to act as though the love of God were real and true and mine—because it is—regardless of how I feel and think.

Practically, this means, first of all, loving myself. Again, if God loves us, the logical conclusion is we ought to love ourselves in response. Loving myself means taking care of myself with that "selfless self-preservation" we talked about in our discussion of temperance. Then I need to act according to the fact that I am an adopted son of God (Romans 8:15), which means going about my life with confidence, not in my flesh, but in my union with Christ. It requires divine courage based on faith to beat back the despair of sin. But in Christ who has sent his Spirit, we have access to this courage.

God's love for us is as unchanging as his love for his Son, which is the basis for his love for us. At times we will doubt our love for him and doubt his love for us, but none of that changes his objective affirmation of our existence in this world and the world to come. We are loved. Our duty is to allow God's love to be the model for the virtue of love in all our relationships as best we can in this life, affirming the goodness of others' existence in echo of God's love.

Love unites all the virtues in one goal: the glorification of God. As we practice love, we cultivate the other virtues as well so that over time the truly just person is the person who loves. The truly temperate person is the person who loves. As the apostle Paul says in 1 Corinthians 13:2, "If I have all faith, so as to remove mountains, but have not love, I am nothing." We cultivate our love by looking to the source of all love, God. By dwelling in his Word, by meditating on his works of love. By being grateful for his acts of love in our lives. And by choosing to love him and our neighbor daily through our attention and our sacrifices with the help of the Holy Spirit.

As we grow in love, we grow in sanctification and into who God created us to be, fully human. This is the goal of the virtues, to help us achieve human excellence, which we must define as God's creational design. But the reality for all of us is that we will never attain that excellence in this life. We will never love fully, completely, genuinely until our final glorification when Christ sanctifies us. Until then, we must follow the model of the apostle Paul: "Brothers, I do not consider that I have made it my own. But one thing I do: forgetting what lies behind and straining forward to what lies ahead, I press on toward the goal for the prize of the upward call of God in Christ Jesus" (Philippians 3:13-14).

CONCLUSION

As society continues to spin away from any sort of central moral standard, and as norms continue to shift, we will continue to feel an aching anxiety about what it means to live as a full human person. We have all lived too long with the "heap of broken images"[1] of a civilization that was far from perfect but did assume a sense of order and direction for humanity, particularly through a shared moral order in the Christian church. This order taught that humans were created to know God and enjoy him forever, and that to love him we must obey his commands, living virtuous lives.

We cannot return to some idyllic past, nor should we desire to, because there is no idyllic past to return to. The past is filled with sins and errors of its own. But we can recover good fragments from the past, pieces of truth, goodness, and beauty that point us to what we were created to be and who we were created to worship. We need to use those fragments to gather our modern lives so that we aren't drifting endlessly from one trend to another, from one job to another, from one relationship to another, from one faith to another, from one diagnosis to another, from one anxiety to another. And the seven virtues are keys to doing this work of gathering, of reforming ourselves, and redirecting our wills toward what God designed us to be.

The virtues demand much of us, but they give much more. In a time of uncertainty, they give us a way of moving through the world with confidence. Justice has a definition; it is not subject to the whims of trending topics on social media or the emotions of millions of people. We are not free to define justice however we want or excuse injustice, but we also don't have to live with the anxiety of justice being whatever the majority finds offensive at the time. The cosmos has an order, defined by God, and the virtues help orient us toward that order. They give us true hope in a time of despair and false hope. And they teach us to love when the word "love" has all but lost its meaning.

COMMUNITY

One difficulty we have not considered in our exploration of the virtues is the problem of the state. In his foundational work on the four cardinal virtues, *Nicomachean Ethics*, Aristotle argues that virtues must be learned from the state through the force of law: "legislators must, in some people's view, urge people toward virtue and exhort them to aim at the fine—on the assumption that anyone whose good habits have prepared him decently will listen to them."[2] In order to be a virtuous person, you need to already have good character so that you are receptive to the virtues, which requires moral education and formation from the broader community.

For Aristotle, this primarily means the state. As you can imagine, or perhaps as you've experienced, moral formation by our government is either woefully inadequate or perverse. In either case it's a bad idea. In his book *The Theory and Practice of Virtue*, Gilbert C. Meilaender writes that within liberal political communities like our own (liberal in the sense of liberty) where there is less and less moral consensus, "most attempts at moral education . . . are likely to be either methods of indoctrination under the guise of moral neutrality or pale imitations of anything that might seriously be called moral education."[3] At best our schools can form some basic civic virtues like patriotism, at worst they indoctrinate a secular progressive ideology which is at odds with our faith.

Meilaender goes on to note that Aristotle accounted for this possibility in his *Ethics*, that some states may not be able to provide the communal formation of virtues necessary, and his solution is that we must work as small communities of families and friends to inculcate the virtues in one another. Aristotle writes: "It is best, then, if the community attends to upbringing, and attends correctly. But if the community neglects it, it seems fitting for each individual to promote the virtue of his children and his friends."[4]

Meilaender is concerned with how to practically develop the virtues in a country like America where there is no moral consensus, where the schools are woefully inadequate for developing virtues and character, and where our laws do not "urge people toward virtue." He argues:

> We should . . . recognize that in political communities like ours, communities which rightly have high regard for individual freedom and which—perhaps because they do so value freedom—lack much in the way of moral consensus, we should be frankly sectarian in our attempts at moral education. Each should help his children and friends strive for virtue as we fashion our smaller communities of belief and seek to transmit the vision which inspires us.[5]

Much of this book has been focused on what it looks like for the individual to practice the seven virtues, but the reality is that they must be practiced in community for them to take root.

As we discussed with prudence, the virtue is found in community, not in isolation. We know *with* each other to get to the truth. When we pursue justice, we do so in community, with other people, for other people, and toward other people (in that sense *all* justice is social justice). The fortitude life demands of us is possible only with a community to supplement our courage, to encourage us when times inevitably get difficult. In temperance we seek to order our lives rightly so that we can better love God and our neighbor.

Our faith is communal; we receive it from those who came before us, we pass it to those who come after us, we share it with those who live with us. We strengthen those who are doubting in their faith and walk with those who are struggling. We practice hope weekly in church, worshiping together, remembering all that God has done for us, and hoping together for what God will do when Christ comes again. And love itself is communal. It is defined by its focus on others. Love cannot be practiced alone. It always develops in community, even if only the community of marriage or friendship. Each of the virtues is dependent on community for its cultivation, and we cannot rely on the state or culture to provide us the ideal conditions to inspire these virtues, especially in the young or those who are hesitant or skeptical about them.

But the Christian has a built-in community in which to practice them: the local church. Families, friends, private schools, and churches ought to be spaces where virtues are openly encouraged. As Meilaender says, we ought to be sectarian, embracing our specific vision of the virtues grounded in the good as defined by God, and raise our children and exhort our friends according to that vision. Meilaender hopes that "out of such sectarianism there will arise some smaller communities whose vision is so powerful and persuasive that new moral consensus will be achieved among us."[6]

Whether we can in fact create a momentum shift in the wider culture toward a moral consensus based on God's vision of the good, we have a responsibility to build spaces of virtue formation in our spheres of influence.

Practically, this looks like using the language of virtue and setting expectations of virtuous behavior. For example, with my children, when they are scared, I acknowledge their feelings, but admonish them to be courageous, to do hard things, to face their fears and overcome them. This helps them build resilience while not dismissing their real feelings. I often talk to them about how our feelings can be there, but they don't have to be in charge of our choices.

When someone comes to me who is distressed and suffering from *acedia*, I help them see that they are falling into despair, that their worth is already established in Christ, and that there is reason to hope. When someone comes to me who has doubts about passages in the Bible, sometimes I help them interpret the passage better, putting it in historical or theological context, sometimes I point them to scholars who can help them answer their questions, but other times I stress the importance of faith. In each of these cases, I use the language of virtues to help me communicate how to respond to a crisis in the world, and that language helps my community develop virtues of their own.

Churches are best equipped to cultivate the three theological virtues: faith, hope, and love. Any church doing the work of preaching the gospel and administering the sacraments will be encouraging these virtues to some extent. But the Bible also has a lot to say about prudence, justice, courage, and temperance. Recovering the language of the virtues in churches would be valuable. The goal here is not to set up "good works" for us to take pride in, but to remind us of what we were created for: "For we are his workmanship, created in Christ Jesus for good works, which God prepared beforehand, that we should walk in them" (Ephesians 2:10).

We were created for good works. We were created to live virtuous lives. God prepared those good works beforehand, so they are not to our credit, so people can't boast in their works, but we still have a duty to walk in those good works. We were not called to passively stumble into good works whenever they might appear, but to actively pursue the good works which "God prepared beforehand, that we *should* walk in them." And we should. Not because in living a virtuous life we gain God's favor, earn our righteousness, or merit our worth, but because this is what we were created to do; because in dying on the cross, Christ gave us the freedom from the bondage to sin so that we can choose righteousness; and because we already have God's favor through grace.

Whether it's through a formal institution like the local church or in the family or a group of friends, as Aristotle exhorts us, we have an opportunity to promote the virtues in those around us. And as we have seen, that is the only way virtues will really be cultivated. What's encouraging to consider are C. S. Lewis's words in *The Four Loves* on the power of just such groups of likeminded friends: "[M]odern attempts to 'sell' Christianity as a means of 'saving civilization,' do not come to much. The little knots of Friends who turn their backs on the 'World' are those who really transform it."[7]

FAILURE

If in the course of reading this book you felt yourself nodding your head but overwhelmed by the prospect of rising to the standard presented by the virtues, I understand. Yes, they are inspiring, but who can live by them? Who can have the courage to be magnanimous? How can I live temperately in a world that insists that I give in to my every desire? How can I be prudent when I have so many decisions to make in life and all of them seem to be life defining? And how can I love when everyone I try to love has the world's understanding of love as personal fulfillment in mind? The virtues can become just another way we feel like we are failing at life in the modern world, and the modern world tells us that we are failing at everything (so we should buy something to fix it).

First of all, it's worth stepping back and acknowledging that the virtues are hard to practice. All of us fail at righteousness in this life based on our own works, but God looks at us based on the righteousness of his Son, Jesus. So our worth is never based on our ability to master the virtues. Our desire in studying and cultivating the virtues is to grow in godliness, as Peter admonishes us in 2 Peter 1:6. And our motivation is gratitude for Christ's completed work on the cross, to which we contribute nothing with our virtues. This is a lifetime's effort, and it involves failures, setbacks, successes, and gains.

But most of all, it involves the struggle, the fight to gain what is worth fighting for: a life well lived for the glory of God and the love of your neighbor. Here the virtues of courage and hope can aid us. In hope we know if we believe that Christ is Lord and have been baptized in the triune name of God, then Christ will finish the good work he began in us, no matter how well we excel at living virtuously (Philippians 1:6). So in courage and magnanimity we walk boldly as adopted sons and daughters of God into life, praying for the work of the Holy Spirit to bend our wills to pursue righteousness, cultivating habits of virtue as best we can, and delighting in the goodness of this life God has blessed us with.

John Calvin is helpful on this point in his *Institutes*:

> Let every one of us go as far as his humble ability enables him, and prosecute the journey once begun. No one will travel so badly as not daily to make some degree of progress.

> This, therefore, let us never cease to do, that we may daily advance in the way of the Lord; and let us not despair because of the slender measure of success. How little soever the success may correspond with our wish, our labor is not lost when today is better than yesterday, provided with true singleness of mind we keep our aim, and aspire to the goal, not speaking flattering things to ourselves, nor indulging our vices, but making it our constant endeavor to become better, until we attain to goodness itself. If during the whole course of our life we seek and follow, we shall at length attain it, when relieved from the infirmity of flesh we are admitted to full fellowship with God.[8]

For Calvin, the emphasis is on faithful perseverance day by day and confidence in God to sanctify us. As T. S. Eliot describes it, such faithfulness is "a lifetime's death in love, / Ardour and selflessness and self-surrender."[9] And it's worth every moment.

Second, it's neither healthy nor appropriate to think of cultivating the virtues in terms of a program or *technique* which will allow us to master our lives. A number of great people have tried to turn the virtues into a method for optimizing their lives, most famously, Benjamin Franklin. In his *Autobiography of Benjamin Franklin*, Franklin set out a chart with each of the virtues he planned to master, and then worked on one of them a day. His goal was to master them one at a time (his list included *thirteen* virtues, not seven), until he had completed the list, and then start over. What he quickly discovered was that overcoming vice is harder work than it seems. His efficient system failed him, as all efficient systems for achieving moral mastery of the self inevitably will.

In the end, the virtues give us a language to talk about the moral *telos* we should strive toward as humans. The work of striving cannot be programmed, although it can be aided and supported. For example, as we discussed earlier, churches and friends can do much to encourage the virtues. Similarly, good stories and art can inspire virtues in people (consider how much *The Lord of the Rings* has to teach us about hope or fortitude, or any of the virtues for that matter!). Perhaps the best we can do to develop the virtues in others is to model it ourselves, which isn't a program, it's a way of life, a day-by-day, decision-by-decision choice to act in accordance with the good, which is God's will. In other words, if you desire to cultivate the virtues in yourself or others, downloading a habit-forming app is not going to help you, but finding the right mentor to model yourself after might. But most important is making the existential choice each day to strive toward virtue while humbly relying on the work of the Holy Spirit in your life.

Third, our habits can't shield us from our propensity to sin. We have seen that for each virtue, society will work against us, inviting us toward vice and the illusion of an easy life (it is only an illusion, because the life of vice is always bitter and rocky). As you grow in virtue, do not expect the pull to vice to disappear. While our virtues and vices are habitual, our fleshly sin nature will overcome our habituated virtues and tempt us to fall back into vice.

For example, if after years of a pornography addiction, you learn through prayer and discipline and mentorship to cultivate the habit of chastity and you no longer look at porn, when the opportunity arises to look lustfully on a beautiful woman, you will be tempted to fall back into that old vice of unchastity. As good and noble as the virtues are, they do not replace the moment-by-moment decisions to turn from sin and choose righteousness. In fact, they *are* the moment-by-moment decisions to turn from sin and choose righteousness. What they are *not* is a kind of automatic pilot we can develop that frees us from the responsibility to think and choose. Although it is true that habits, whether good or bad, make it easier for us to choose a specific path, we still must ultimately choose. Christ's finished work on the cross enables us to choose righteousness, instead of sin. Sometimes we will fail and choose sin despite the freedom we have in Christ, and for that, there is grace.

GRACE

The end of all virtues is love, and the manifestation of love from God toward us is grace. By grace God created us. By grace he sustains us. By grace he saved us. While it is beautiful and good to pursue these virtues, they neither save us nor define our worth. When God looks upon us, he sees the righteousness of his Son and is pleased. We live by grace.

And that grace frees us from the burden of striving for earthly mastery of ourselves for the sake of ourselves. Many YouTube and Instagram gurus offer people, particularly young men, guides to self-mastery through fitness, finance, and self-denial, but their vision of self-mastery is hedonistic, self-centered, and exhausting. It is a vision with no space for grace or mercy, only more stringent discipline. But God's grace allows us to pursue the virtues with the freedom to make mistakes, to strive and fail at times, to wrestle and ultimately *rest in God's mercy.*

No matter how virtuous you are, you need God's mercy. You need to rest in God's mercy. When you lie down at night, the hope that gives you peace to sleep is not your virtuous works, but God's loving grace to you. You can sleep the sleep of the righteous because you are righteous before God. And when you wake up in the morning, your duty is to strive for a virtuous life, not so that you can earn a peaceful night's sleep (although a life of vice will disturb your sleep), but because it's delightful and good to embrace the way of life God has created you to live. You were made to be virtuous.

Yes, we have only known a heap of broken images, moral fragments from a society at war with itself, but by turning to the good embodied in God and grounding ourselves in the virtues as guides, we can gather up the good fragments and navigate the chaos of our times. We do this work of gathering fragments together in community, particularly in the church. And we are enabled to do this work through the indwelling power of the Holy Spirit. As a body, we piece together the redeemable fragments, encouraging each other in Christ to love and good works, and to persevere through the pressures to turn back to vices.

What we discover through this work is that these fragments are part of a coherent whole. That they are not random, subjective, or relative, but that they make up a beautiful stained-glass window created by God. There is order, unity, meaning, purpose, mystery, and direction to the flow of life despite the feeling of chaos and uncertainty presented by the contemporary world. The order of life is God's creational design for humans and his cosmic plan of redemption. As we have seen, the virtues help us practice that order insofar as they are oriented toward God. And the exciting thing is we were made to participate in the story depicted in this beautiful stained-glass window. Not because we are particularly virtuous, but because God loves us and died for us. And that is a good reason to act virtuously.

Near the end of his earthly ministry, Christ spoke to his disciples about the signs of his returning. He warned of "people fainting with fear and with foreboding of what is coming on the world" (Luke 21:26). That kind of anxiety about the future certainly describes our own highly anxious and chaotic age, people uncertain of what is true and what is safe and what is coming. In response to this anxiety, Christ tells his disciples, "When these things begin to take place, straighten up and raise your heads, because your redemption is drawing near" (Luke 21:28). In the end, that is why we act virtuously, because our redemption is secure and at hand. The end is written for us in Christ. So let us straighten up and raise our heads confidently, walking steadfastly into our inheritance.

ACKNOWLEDGMENTS

I'D LIKE TO THANK Brittany, Nora, Quentin, and Franny for their sacrifices that made this book possible. Don Gates for his advocacy. Ethan McCarthy for his encouragement. Derek Rishmawy for his prayers and encouragement. Rya'lynn Simons for her help. My many friends in Nashville for their hospitality during the summer of 2023, when this book was just getting started. Oklahoma Baptist University for a sabbatical that helped me write and revise this book, and for their continued support of my writing. The Keller Fellows and MereOrthodoxy for being supportive groups of Christian intellectuals who I can bounce ideas off of. Josef Pieper for his work. And most of all, to God for giving me this opportunity. I pray it does some good.

NOTES

INTRODUCTION

[1] T. S. Eliot, "The Waste Land," *The Poems of T. S. Eliot*, ed. Christopher Ricks and Jim McCue, vol. 1 (Farrar, Straus and Giroux, 2015), 55.

[2] "The Westminster Shorter Catechism," The Presbytery of the United States, The Free Church of Scotland (Continuing), December 11, 2023, www.westminsterconfession.org/resources/confessional-standards/the-westminster-shorter-catechism/.

[3] For more on Pieper's life under Nazi rule, see Jon Vickery, "Searching for Josef Pieper," *Theological Studies* 66, no. 3 (September 2005): 622-37, https://doi.org/10.1177/004056390506600307.

[4] Josef Pieper, *The Four Cardinal Virtues* (University of Notre Dame Press, 2010), xiii.

[5] Josef Pieper, *Faith, Hope, Love* (Ignatius Press, 2012), 174, emphasis in original.

[6] Kevin White, "A Cosmopolitan Hermit: Modernity and Tradition in the Philosophy of Josef Pieper," *Notre Dame Philosophical Reviews*, September 4, 2021, https://ndpr.nd.edu/reviews/a-cosmopolitan-hermit-modernity-and-tradition-in-the-philosophy-of-josef-pieper/.

[7] "My intention, however, in the plan of life which I now propose to give, is not to extent it so far as to treat each virtue specially, and expatiate in exhortation. This must be sought in the writings of others, and particularly in the homilies of the fathers." John Calvin, *Institutes of the Christian Religion*, trans. Henry Beveridge (Hendrickson Publishers, 2008), 3.6.1.

1. CHOOSING DECISIVELY

[1] T. S. Eliot, "The Waste Land," *The Poems of T. S. Eliot*, ed. Christopher Ricks and Jim McCue, vol. 1 (Farrar, Straus and Giroux, 2015), 55.

[2] W. Jay Wood, "Prudence," in *Virtues and Their Vices*, ed. Kevin Timpe and Craig A. Boyd (Oxford University Press, 2014), 48.

[3] "Of the Morals of the Catholic Church," *Church Fathers: Of the Morals of the Catholic Church (Augustine)*, De Morib. Eccl. 15, accessed August 26, 2025, www.newadvent.org/fathers/1401.htm.

[4] Josef Pieper, *The Four Cardinal Virtues* (University of Notre Dame Press, 2010), 3.

[5] Pieper, *The Four Cardinal Virtues*, 16.

[6] Esther Lightcap Meek, *A Little Manual for Knowing* (Cascade Books, 2014), 68.

[7] I think it's notable here that each of these great thinkers is calling us toward a deeper, more intimate, more honest vision of reality. Sometimes Christianity is depicted as an *escape* from reality, a denial of the natural world and science. Meek seems to imply that it is precisely those who have a narrow scientific (rather than robust) vision of reality as a mass of data who fail to recognize reality as it is.

[8] The implication here is that perfect prudence belongs to Christians who know the good (God). For more, see Aquinas, ST II-II, q. 47, a. 13.

[9] "The Westminster Shorter Catechism," The Presbytery of the United States, The Free Church of Scotland (Continuing), December 11, 2023, www.westminsterconfession.org/resources/confessional-standards/the-westminster-shorter-catechism/.

[10] Pieper, *The Four Cardinal Virtues*, 34, emphasis in original.

[11] Pieper, *The Four Cardinal Virtues*, 34.

[12] "We deliberate about what is up to us, that is to say, about the actions we can do; and this is the remaining possibility." Aristotle, *Nicomachean Ethics*, trans. Terence Irwin, third ed. (Hackett Publishing, 2019), III.3.7.

[13] Wood, "Prudence," 44.

[14] "Prudence concerns particular things to be done. But since there is an almost infinite variety in such things, one human being cannot sufficiently consider all things or consider them in a short span of time. And so, regarding things belonging to prudence, human beings especially need to learn from others, and especially from elders, who have obtained sound understanding of the ends of things to be done, And it belongs to the disposition to learn that one receive instruction well." Aquinas, *The Cardinal Virtues: Prudence, Justice, Fortitude, and Temperance*, trans. and ed. Richard J. Regan (Hackett Publishing Company, 2005), ST II-II, q. 49, a. 3.

[15] Pieper, *The Four Cardinal Virtues*, 29.

[16] Meek, *A Little Manual for Knowing*, 42.

[17] Wood, "Prudence," 42.

[18] Wood, "Prudence," 46.

[19] Pieper, *The Four Cardinal Virtues*, 18.

[20] Wood, "Prudence," 42.

[21] "A Christian directory, or, A summm of practical theologie and cases of conscience directing Christians how to use their knowledge and faith, how to improve all helps and means, and to perform all duties, how to overcome temptations, and to escape or mortifie every sin : in four parts . . . / by Richard Baxter." In the digital collection Early English Books Online Collections, 448, accessed December 31, 2024, https://name.umdl.umich.edu/A26892.0001.001, emphasis in original.

[22] You can find a similar list in the book *Every Good Endeavor* (Penguin Books, 2012) by Timothy Keller and Katherine Leary Alsdorf. I can't say if I was inspired by Keller and Alsdorf or just came to the same theological conclusions independently. Either way, I think it's a good list.

[23] Pieper, *The Four Cardinal Virtues*, 18.

2. ACTING JUSTLY

[1] Jade S. Sasser, "'It's Almost Shameful to Want to Have Children,'" *Los Angeles Times*, September 11, 2024, www.latimes.com/environment/story/2024-09-11/climate-anxiety-and-the-kid-question.

[2] Alasdair MacIntyre, *After Virtue*, third ed. (University of Notre Dame Press, 2007), 11-12.

[3] T. S. Eliot, "The Waste Land," *The Poems of T. S. Eliot*, ed. Christopher Ricks and Jim McCue, vol. 1 (Farrar, Straus and Giroux, 2015), 55.

[4] Josef Pieper, *The Four Cardinal Virtues* (University of Notre Dame Press, 2010), 44.

[5] Pieper, *The Four Cardinal Virtues*, 44.

[6] Pieper, *The Four Cardinal Virtues*, 51.

[7] Pieper, *The Four Cardinal Virtues*, 60-61.

[8] Pieper, *The Four Cardinal Virtues*, 63.

[9] Pieper, *The Four Cardinal Virtues*, 62, emphasis in original.

[10] Pieper, *The Four Cardinal Virtues*, 95.

[11] Pieper, *The Four Cardinal Virtues*, 99.

[12] John Calvin, *Institutes of the Christian Religion*, trans. Henry Beveridge (Hendrickson Publishers, 2008), 3.7.4.

[13] Pieper, *The Four Cardinal Virtues*, 80.

[14] Pieper, *The Four Cardinal Virtues*, 80.

[15] Pieper, *The Four Cardinal Virtues*, 80.

[16] Pieper, *The Four Cardinal Virtues*, 112, emphasis in original.

[17] Pieper, *The Four Cardinal Virtues*, 105, emphasis in original.

[18] Pieper, *The Four Cardinal Virtues*, 110-11.

[19] Pieper, *The Four Cardinal Virtues*, 111.

[20] Alan Noble, *You Are Not Your Own: Belonging to God in an Inhuman World* (Inter-Varsity Press, 2021).

[21] See, for example, Thomas Aquinas, *Summa Theologica*, II-II, q. 32, a. 5, and John Calvin's *Institutes*: "We shall thus succeed in mortifying ourselves if we fulfill all the duties of charity" (3.7.7).

[22] Calvin, *Institutes*, 3.7.7.

[23] William Faulker, *Requiem for a Nun* (Vintage International, 2011), 73.

[24] T. S. Eliot, "Choruses from 'The Rock,'" in *Collected Poems 1909–1962* (Harcourt Inc., 1991), 153.

[25] Eliot, "Choruses from 'The Rock,'" 153.

3. SUFFERING STEADFASTLY

[1] Josef Pieper, *The Four Cardinal Virtues* (University of Notre Dame Press, 2010), 117.

[2] "About Mental Health," U.S. Centers for Disease Control and Prevention, 2025, www.cdc.gov/mental-health/about/index.html.

[3] Dan Witters, "U.S. Depression Rates Reach New Highs," Gallup.com, March 26, 2025, https://news.gallup.com/poll/505745/depression-rates-reach-new-highs.aspx.

[4] Alain Ehrenberg, *The Weariness of the Self: Diagnosing the History of Depression in the Contemporary Age* (McGill-Queen's University Press, 2016), 166.

[5] Jacques Ellul, *The Technological Society*, trans. John Wilkinson (Vintage Books, 1964).

[6] See especially the work of Jonathan Haidt and Greg Lukianoff, *The Coddling of the American Mind: How Good Intentions and Bad Ideas Are Setting Up a Generation for Failure* (Penguin Press, 2018), and Haidt's more recent work, *The Anxious Generation* (Penguin Press, 2024).

[7] T. S. Eliot, "The Waste Land," *The Poems of T. S. Eliot*, ed. Christopher Ricks and Jim McCue, vol. 1 (Farrar, Straus and Giroux, 2015), 55.

[8] See Robert Bellah and his coauthors' *Habits of the Heart* (HarperCollins, 1985) and Charles Taylor's *A Secular Age* (Belknap Press, 2007).

[9] Pieper, *The Four Cardinal Virtues*, 117.

[10] Pieper, *The Four Cardinal Virtues*, 118.

[11] Pieper, *The Four Cardinal Virtues*, 119.

[12] Pieper, *The Four Cardinal Virtues*, 123.

[13] Pieper, *The Four Cardinal Virtues*, 125.

14 Pieper, *The Four Cardinal Virtues*, 126.

15 Thomas Aquinas, *Summa Theologica*, II-II, q. 123, a. 6.

16 Pieper, *The Four Cardinal Virtues*, 128.

17 Cormac McCarthy, *The Road* (Vintage International, 2006), 54.

18 Richard Fry, "Rising Share of U.S. Adults Are Living without a Spouse or Partner," Pew Research Center, October 5, 2021, www.pewresearch.org/social-trends/2021/10/05/rising-share-of-u-s-adults-are-living-without-a-spouse-or-partner/.

19 Wendy Wang, "The U.S. Marriage Rate Rebounds to Its Pre-Pandemic Level," Institute for Family Studies, September 15, 2023, https://ifstudies.org/blog/the-us-marriage-rate-rebounds-to-its-pre-pandemic-level.

20 C. S. Lewis, *The Four Loves* (HarperCollins, 1960), 155-56.

21 Aristotle, *Nicomachean Ethics*, trans. Terence Irwin, third ed. (Hackett Publishing, 2019), IV.3.1.

22 "The magnanimous person, then, seems to be the one who thinks himself worthy of great things and is really worthy of them. For if someone is not worthy of them but thinks he is, he is foolish, and no virtuous person is foolish or senseless; hence the magnanimous person is the one we have mentioned." Aristotle, *Nicomachean Ethics*, IV.3.3.

23 Aristotle, *Nicomachean Ethics*, IV.3.35.

24 "Magnanimity, then, would seem to be a sort of adornment of the virtues; for it makes them greater, and it does not arise without them. That is why it is difficult to be truly magnanimous, since it is not possible without being fine and good." Aristotle, *Nicomachean Ethics*, IV.3.16.

4. LIVING MODERATELY

1 Alain Ehrenberg, *The Weariness of the Self: Diagnosing the History of Depression in the Contemporary Age* (McGill-Queen's University Press, 2010), 232.

2 Dan Witters, "U.S. Depression Rates Reach New Highs," Gallup.com, March 26, 2025, https://news.gallup.com/poll/505745/depression-rates-reach-new-highs.aspx.

3 "NIDA IC Fact Sheet 2024," National Institutes of Health, March 13, 2023, https://nida.nih.gov/about-nida/legislative-activities/budget-information/fiscal-year-2024-budget-information-congressional-justification-national-institute-drug-abuse/ic-fact-sheet-2024.

4 Trevor Wheelwright, "Cell Phone Usage Stats 2025: Americans Check Their Phones 205 Times a Day," Reviews.org, January 1, 2025, www.reviews.org/mobile/cell-phone-addiction/.

[5] Joshua P. Cohen, "As Sports Betting Proliferates, Incidence of Gambling Disorder Rises," *Forbes*, May 7, 2024, www.forbes.com/sites/joshuacohen/2024/05/07/as-sports-betting-proliferates-incidence-of-gambling-disorder-rises/.

[6] Alex Shephard, "Our Entire Society Is Becoming Addicted to Sports Gambling," *The New Republic*, April 3, 2024, https://newrepublic.com/article/180373/ohtani-sports-gambling-addiction-crisis.

[7] Brett Hollenbeck et al., "The Financial Consequences of Legalized Sports Gambling," last modified July 23, 2024, *SSRN*, https://ssrn.com/abstract=4903302.

[8] Joshua B. Grubbs et al., "Self-Reported Addiction to Pornography in a Nationally Representative Sample: The Roles of Use Habits, Religiousness, and Moral Incongruence," *Journal of Behavioral Addictions* 8, no. 1 (January 11, 2019): 88-93, https://doi.org/10.1556/2006.7.2018.134.

[9] Bruno Castelo-Branco and Puneet Manchanda, "An Empirical Analysis of Video Game Play and Addiction Patterns," last modified June 1, 2023, http://dx.doi.org/10.2139/ssrn.4714079.

[10] Charles Taylor, *A Secular Age* (Belknap Press, 2007), 489.

[11] T. S. Eliot, "The Waste Land," *The Poems of T. S. Eliot*, ed. Christopher Ricks and Jim McCue, vol. 1 (Farrar, Straus and Giroux, 2015), 55.

[12] Josef Pieper, *The Four Cardinal Virtues* (University of Notre Dame Press, 2010), 146.

[13] Pieper, *The Four Cardinal Virtues*, 147.

[14] Pieper, *The Four Cardinal Virtues*, 147.

[15] Pieper, *The Four Cardinal Virtues*, 148.

[16] Pieper, *The Four Cardinal Virtues*, 148.

[17] Jacques Ellul, "The Ethics of Nonpower," in *Ethics in an Age of Pervasive Technology*, ed. Melvin Kranzberg (Routledge, 1980), 193, Kindle.

[18] I first introduced this concept in Alan Noble, *You Are Not Your Own: Belonging to God in an Inhuman World* (InterVarsity Press, 2021). This is an explication of that idea.

[19] Bobby Allyn et al., "TikTok Executives Know About App's Effect on Teens, Lawsuit Documents Allege," NPR, October 11, 2024, www.npr.org/2024/10/11/g-s1-27676/tiktok-redacted-documents-in-teen-safety-lawsuit-revealed.

[20] Pieper, *The Four Cardinal Virtues*, 204-5.

[21] Pieper, *The Four Cardinal Virtues*, 161.

5. BELIEVING SOUNDLY

[1] T. S. Eliot, "Little Gidding," *The Poems of T. S. Eliot*, ed. Christopher Ricks and Jim McCue, vol. 1 (Farrar, Straus and Giroux, 2015), 209.

[2] Charles Taylor, *A Secular Age* (Belknap Press, 2007), 556.

[3] Josef Pieper, *Faith, Hope, Love* (Ignatius Press, 2012), 24.

[4] Pieper, *Faith, Hope, Love*, 30.

[5] John Calvin, *Institutes of the Christian Religion*, trans. Henry Beveridge (Hendrickson Publishers, 2008), 3.2.7.

[6] Pieper, *Faith, Hope, Love*, 33.

[7] Pieper, *Faith, Hope, Love*, 37.

[8] Pieper, *Faith, Hope, Love*, 37.

[9] Pieper, *Faith, Hope, Love*, 47, emphasis in original.

[10] Calvin, *Institutes*, 3.2.17.

[11] Calvin, *Institutes*, 3.2.17.

[12] Calvin, *Institutes*, 3.2.19.

[13] Eliot, "Little Gidding," 208.

[14] Credit for this section goes to my wife, Brittany.

6. HOPING RESOLUTELY

[1] Jacques Ellul, *Hope in Time of Abandonment*, trans. C. Edward Hopkin (Wipf and Stock, 2012), 7.

[2] Ellul, *Hope in Time of Abandonment*, 8.

[3] Leah Ginsberg, "Elon Musk Thinks Life on Earth Will Go Extinct, and Is Putting Most of His Fortune Toward Colonizing Mars," CNBC, June 16, 2017, www.cnbc.com/2017/06/16/elon-musk-colonize-mars-before-extinction-event-on-earth.html.

[4] Josef Pieper, *Faith, Hope, Love* (Ignatius Press, 2012), 100.

[5] Pieper, *Faith, Hope, Love*, 105.

[6] Pieper, *Faith, Hope, Love*, 107.

[7] Pieper, *Faith, Hope, Love*, 106.

[8] Pieper, *Faith, Hope, Love*, 107.

[9] Pieper, *Faith, Hope, Love*, 113.

[10] Pieper, *Faith, Hope, Love*, 113.

[11] Charlotte Alter, "Bryan Johnson's Quest for Immortality," Time, September 20, 2023, https://time.com/6315607/bryan-johnsons-quest-for-immortality/.

[12] Pieper, *Faith, Hope, Love*, 114.

[13] Pieper, *Faith, Hope, Love*, 114.

[14] Pieper, *Faith, Hope, Love*, 115.

[15] Pieper, *Faith, Hope, Love*, 116.

[16] Pieper, *Faith, Hope, Love*, 117.

[17] Pieper, *Faith, Hope, Love*, 118.

[18] Pieper, *Faith, Hope, Love*, 119.

[19] Pieper, *Faith, Hope, Love*, 118.

[20] Pieper, *Faith, Hope, Love*, 118.

[21] Pieper, *Faith, Hope, Love*, 120.

[22] T. S. Eliot, "Little Gidding," *The Poems of T. S. Eliot*, ed. Christopher Ricks and Jim McCue, vol. 1 (Farrar, Straus and Giroux, 2015), 207.

[23] T. S. Eliot, "East Coker," *The Poems of T. S. Eliot*, ed. Christopher Ricks and Jim McCue, vol. 1 (Farrar, Straus and Giroux, 2015), 189.

7. LOVING RIGHTLY

[1] T. S. Eliot, "The Waste Land," *The Poems of T. S. Eliot*, ed. Christopher Ricks and Jim McCue, vol. 1 (Farrar, Straus and Giroux, 2015), 55.

[2] Charles Taylor, *A Secular Age* (Belknap Press, 2007), 489.

[3] Josef Pieper, *Faith, Hope, Love* (Ignatius Press, 2012), 163-64.

[4] Pieper, *Faith, Hope, Love*, 171, emphasis in original.

[5] Pieper, *Faith, Hope, Love*, 164.

[6] Pieper, *Faith, Hope, Love*, 187-88, emphasis in original.

[7] Pieper, *Faith, Hope, Love*, 188.

[8] Pieper, *Faith, Hope, Love*, 188, emphasis in original.

[9] Pieper, *Faith, Hope, Love*, 188.

[10] Pieper, *Faith, Hope, Love*, 188-189.

[11] Pieper, *Faith, Hope, Love*, 188.

[12] Pieper, *Faith, Hope, Love*, 190.

[13] Pieper, *Faith, Hope, Love*, 170.

[14] Pieper, *Faith, Hope, Love*, 205.

[15] Pieper, *Faith, Hope, Love*, 172.

[16] Pieper, *Faith, Hope, Love*, 176.

[17] Pieper, *Faith, Hope, Love*, 163-64.

[18] Saint Augustine, *The Works of Saint Augustine: A Translation for the 21st Century*, trans. Edmund Hill, ed. John E. Rotelle, pt. 3, vol. 10 (New City Press, 1995), 302.

[19] Pieper, *Faith, Hope, Love*, 237.

[20] Pieper, *Faith, Hope, Love*, 174, emphasis in original.

[21] Aristotle, *Nicomachean Ethics*, trans. Terence Irwin, third ed. (Hackett Publishing, 2019), VIII.3.1-8.

[22] Aristotle, *Nicomachean Ethics*, VIII.1.1.

[23] C. S. Lewis, *The Four Loves* (HarperCollins, 1960), 74.

[24] Office of the Surgeon General, "Our Epidemic of Loneliness and Isolation," US Department of Health and Human Services, 2023, www.hhs.gov/sites/default/files/surgeon-general-social-connection-advisory.pdf.

25 Daniel A. Cox, "The State of American Friendship: Change, Challenges, and Loss—the Survey Center on American Life," The Survey Center on American Life, June 8, 2021, www.americansurveycenter.org/research/the-state-of-american-friendship-change-challenges-and-loss/.

26 Lewis, *The Four Loves*, 78.

CONCLUSION

1 T. S. Eliot, "The Waste Land," *The Poems of T. S. Eliot*, ed. Christopher Ricks and Jim McCue, vol. 1 (Farrar, Straus and Giroux, 2015), 55.

2 Aristotle, *Nicomachean Ethics*, trans. Terence Irwin, third ed. (Hackett Publishing, 2019), X.9.10.

3 Gilbert C. Meilaender, *The Theory and Practice of Virtue* (University of Notre Dame Press, 1984), 98.

4 Aristotle, *Nicomachean Ethics*, X.9.14.

5 Meilaender, *The Theory and Practice of Virtue*, 98.

6 Meilaender, *The Theory and Practice of Virtue*, 98.

7 C. S. Lewis, *The Four Loves* (HarperCollins, 1960), 88.

8 John Calvin, *Institutes of the Christian Religion*, trans. Henry Beveridge (Hendrickson Publishers, 2008), 3.6.5.

9 T. S. Eliot, "The Dry Salvages," *The Poems of T. S. Eliot*, ed. Christopher Ricks and Jim McCue, vol. 1 (Farrar, Straus and Giroux, 2015), 200.

ALSO BY THE AUTHOR

Disruptive Witness
978-0-8308-4483-8

You Are Not Your Own
978-1-5140-1095-2

On Getting Out of Bed
978-1-5140-0443-2